Must
Year

Must Year

Your Best Year of Becoming

365-Day Journey of Identity,
Growth, and Habits

STEPHEN RUE

Award Winning, Best Selling Author

MUST BOOK PRESS

COPYRIGHT © 2025 Stephen Rue

All rights reserved.

MUST YEAR
Your Best Year of Becoming – A 365-Day Journey of Identity, Growth, and Habits

FIRST EDITION

ISBN: 979-8-9935336-3-6   Hardback
ISBN: 979-8-9935336-4-3   Paperback
ISBN: 979-8-9935336-5-0   E-Book

CONTENTS

Dedication vii
Before You Begin xi
Introduction xiii
How To Use This Book xix
The Must Circle of Life xxv
My Beginning Identity Statement xxvii

Season 1 – Waking Up to Your Life (Days 1–90) 1
   Season 1 Overview: Becoming Awake to Yourself 1
   Quarter 1 – Waking Up to Your Life 93
Season 2 – Practicing New Ways of Being (Days 91–180) ... 95
   Season 2 Overview: Experiments, Boundaries &
   Small Bravery 95
   Quarter 2 – Practicing New Ways of Being 186
Season 3 – Integrating a Whole Life 189
   Season 3 Overview: Alignment, Insight & Identity
   Consolidation 189
   Quarter 3 – Integrating a Whole Life 280
Season 4 – Closing and Beginning (Days 271–360) 283
   Season 4 Overview: Review, Release & Forward Intention 284
   Quarter 4 – Closing and Beginning 380

A Year-End Letter 383
Thank you, and Next Steps 387
Acknowledgments 389
If You Want to Go Further: The Must Personal
Development Series 391
Recommended Reading and Resources 393
About The Author 395

DEDICATION

To the one holding this book—the kindred spirit who refuses to drift through life on autopilot, who feels that inner pull to grow, to heal, and to step more fully into who you are meant to become, for your sake and for the sake of the ones you love.

To the soul who keeps showing up, even when it is inconvenient, lonely, or slow… who dares to look honestly at your own heart and still chooses the path of transformation.

This book is for you—
the one courageous enough to live your life as a Must.

BEFORE YOU BEGIN

*A gentle orientation
to the year that is about to change you.*

Before you turn to Day 1, pause for a moment. Something brought you here—an ache for clarity, a hunger for change, a quiet knowing that you cannot keep living as the smaller version of yourself you had to become to survive. You're not holding a productivity tool or a motivation manual. **You're holding a year-long homecoming.**

A *Must Year* is not about adding more to your life. It is about **returning to the truth of who you are**—the person you were meant to become long before expectations, roles, and survival shaped you into someone smaller.

Most people try to change their life by fixing the visible habits. But you are not here for surface. You are here for identity. **Identity is the engine of everything that lasts.** When you shift the story of who you believe you are, your habits follow. Your choices follow. Your relationships, your boundaries, your energy, your money, your joy, your peace—all of it begins to align.

This book guides you through nine essential domains, revisiting them again and again the way a wise teacher or loving friend would: steadily and gently, not letting you turn away from the truth. You won't be asked to become perfect. You will be asked to become honest. Because honesty is where transformation finally begins to breathe.

A *Must Year* doesn't care if you get ahead or fall behind. It doesn't matter if you simply reflect, write a paragraph, or a single shaky sentence. It doesn't matter if you miss days or start over in the middle. It cares about one thing only:

You came back.

Every time you return—after chaos, after distraction, after doubt—you strengthen something in you that has been waiting for this exact kind of attention.

As the days unfold, pay attention to the subtle shifts:
the new way you talk to yourself,
the boundary you didn't apologize for,
the breath you took,
the moment you saw your life with clearer eyes,
the quiet courage that surprised even you.

These shifts are not small. These incremental shifts are the first signs of real change.

By the end of this year, you may still be facing challenges, but you will not face them as the person who began these pages. You will face them with deeper truth, steadier identity, and a self-respect that cannot be undone.

This is the real promise of a *Must Year*:
not that your life will look different, but that you will.
And once you change, the life that fits your identity begins to rise to meet you.

Welcome. Your year of becoming has already begun.

INTRODUCTION

You are holding a year-long conversation with yourself.

Not the version of you who is merely trying to get more done, earn a little more, or patch a few habits. The version of you who knows, somewhere underneath the noise, that life is meant to be lived as a Must—not a maybe, not a "someday," not a compromise you learn to tolerate. This book is a guided year to become that Must self, one honest question at a time.

What This Book Is (and Is Not)

This is not a resolution book.

Resolutions are usually about outcomes: lose the weight, fix the debt, publish the thing, be less this, more that. They tend to flare, fade, and leave you with the same identity you started with—just a little more tired and self-critical.

The *Must Year* is different. It is a re-introduction to who you are meant to be.

Across 365 days, you will stay in conversation with the most important parts of your life:

- Your health and vitality.
- Your career and financial well-being.
- Your love and intimacy.
- Your family, friends, and community.
- Your career development and meaningful work.
- Your personal growth and learning.
- Your spirituality and inner peace.
- Your joy, rest, and renewal.
- Your whole-life integration.

You will not visit these once and move on. You will cycle through them repeatedly, from different angles and at different depths—the way a good coach or a lifelong friend would: "Tell me more about this. What's changing here? What do you see now that you couldn't see before?"

The strongest honest promise this book can make is simple: if you stay in conversation with these 365 pages, you will not be the same person at the end of the year—regardless of how much your outer circumstances change.

Why That Promise Is Honest

That promise is not magic. That happens because of how this book was intentionally built.

Repeated cycles through every major life domain

Most people focus too much on one area—usually work or whatever is on fire—and neglect the rest of their life wheel until something breaks. This book keeps gently rotating you through the core domains, so no part of your life has to carry the whole weight for long.

Over time, you begin to see patterns: how money stress affects your sleep, how exhaustion shapes your relationships, how unspoken beliefs about love show up at work, how a lack of play dries out your spiritual life. You start living a whole life, not a collection of disconnected problems.

1. Systematic replacement of old identity scripts

Change that lasts does not start with "What goal do I want?" but with "Who do I believe I am?"

Hidden scripts run in the background:

- "I'm bad with money."
- "I never follow through."
- "I'm the one who has to fix everything."
- "I'm too much."
- "I'm not the kind of person who can do that."

This book does not simply tell you to "think positive." It gives you 365 micro conversations that:

- Expose the old script.
- Offer a more truthful, chosen identity statement.
- Invite one small action that casts a "vote" for that new identity.

Over months, the story you tell about who you are becomes less accidental and more chosen.

2. Concrete work on the hard stuff

A lot of self-development writing stays vague when things get uncomfortable. This one does not.

Across the year you will receive concrete, plain-spoken guidance around:

- **Boundaries:** saying yes and no without constant guilt; distinguishing between walls and doors.
- **Communication:** speaking from needs, not just accusations; checking assumptions; learning repair.
- **Money emotions**: fear, shame, guilt, scarcity, overwork, and the quiet beliefs beneath your decisions.
- **Health shame:** moving from self-contempt to responsible action; respecting limits while stretching.
- **Self-talk:** replacing "I'm hopeless" with "Here's where I am and here's my next honest step."
- **Spiritual honesty:** bringing anger, doubt, and confusion into your reflective or spiritual life instead of trying to "clean yourself up" first.

These are not random questions. They are targeted conversations in the places most people avoid and where most lives are shaped.

3. Built-in seasons of review and integration

Change does not happen in a straight line. You need moments to stop, look back, and see what is shifting.

Scattered throughout the *Must Year* are days that ask you to:

- Review the last week or month.
- Notice what has improved, even slightly.
- Identify repeating lessons.
- Decide what to keep, what to release, and what to try next.

By the final stretch of the year, you will walk through structured end-of-year reflections: gratitude, regrets turned into lessons, what you are leaving behind, and how you intend to live the next chapter. These pages turn daily reflection into a new way of relating to your whole life.

Where This Book Comes From

This book stands on two foundations.

First, it grows out of the Must work: the exploration of Must vs. Should, identity-based goals, and the conviction that you are meant to live as the person you are here to be—not as a smaller version that simply fits everyone else's expectations.

Second, it draws from the distilled insights and wisdom of many modern and historical voices across psychology, neuroscience, behavioral science, spirituality, and lived experience—luminaries and practitioners whose work on change, meaning, and habits has quietly shaped every page of this book.

The *Must Year* is far from random. It is a carefully crafted system of self-discovery and development.

- Each domain appears by design.
- Each topic shows up when it is most useful.
- Each question is chosen to open a specific door in you.

Think of it as a long, honest conversation with a lifelong friend who knows your potential, respects your pain, and is not interested in your excuses.

HOW TO USE THIS BOOK

This book is not here to impress you in one sitting. It is here to stay in conversation with you for a year.

You do not have to use it perfectly, in order, without missing a day. You do not have to write long reflections every time. You do not have to wait for January or a "fresh start Monday." You only must do one thing:

Keep coming back.

The *Must Year* is designed to be flexible, forgiving, and powerful in real life, not in fantasy life. These pages will meet you where you are.

What you will find inside

Each day follows a simple pattern:

- A short reflection about one part of your life.
- One focused question called **Today's Must Reflection**.
- Space for you to respond in your own words, if you choose.

The days rotate through the nine Must domains, with periodic Whole-Life check-ins. Every 90 days, you'll also pause for a *Season Marker* page that names what this season of your *Must Year* is about, so these 365 days never feel like a stack of random pages but a guided arc.

One day at a time

The basic practice is simple:

1. Open to today's page.
2. Read the reflection slowly. Let the ideas land before you decide what you think.
3. Answer **Today's Must Reflection.**

You might:

- Write a few sentences or bullet points.
- On rushed days, write a single honest line.
- On really rushed days, if all you can do is think about the question while you walk or shower, that still counts.

Perfection is not required. Honesty is.

If you miss a day—or a week—do not try to "catch up" by cramming. Simply come back to the next page. The conversation is more important than the streak.

How to begin (anytime)

You can start this book on January 1, on your birthday, or on a random Wednesday.

Because each entry is labeled Day 1, Day 2, and so on (not by calendar date), you are free to begin when you choose:

- If you are starting fresh, begin at Day 1.
- If you are mid-year but drawn to a particular theme (for example, health or money), you may browse the table of contents, find a day that speaks to you, and start there. Then continue forward.

There is no wrong doorway into your own life.

Writing and Reflecting: what "counts"

You may feel pressure to write perfectly crafted answers. Let that go.

In this book:

- A single honest sentence is enough.
- Bullet points are enough.
- "I don't know yet, but I suspect…" is enough.
- "I'm not ready to answer this today" is an honest answer.

Try to write like you talk to someone you trust. This book is a private conversation. No one will grade your grammar, your handwriting, or how "inspiring" you sound. What changes you is not how pretty your words are, but how true they are.

Using the Online Companion Journal

If you prefer to keep this book clean or write on separate pages, you can download a printable companion journal at **MustYear.com/Resources**. The companion PDF gives you organized space for your daily Must reflections, season markers, and year-end reviews, while this book stays as your guide and reference.

About the life domains

As you read, you will see small visual icons are provided for different domains (for example, **Health & Vitality, Career & Financial Well-Being, Love & Intimacy,** and so on). These are ways of organizing your attention.

Over time, you will feel which areas are strong for you and which are asking for more attention.

When it gets uncomfortable

Some days will feel easy. Others will touch tender places: old hurt, regret, fear, shame, anger, or deep desire.

When that happens:

- Pause. Breathe.
- Remind yourself that noticing a feeling is not the same as being ruled by it.
- Write what you can. If you need to stop mid-answer, that is allowed.

If something feels too big to hold alone, consider sharing that page with a trusted friend, mentor, therapist, or spiritual guide. This book is not a substitute for professional support. It is a tool that can make that support deeper, if you choose to bring your reflections into those conversations.

Missed days, busy seasons, and "falling off"

You will miss days. You may miss weeks. You may even put the book down for a season.

When that happens, notice what your old script wants to say:

- "I blew it."
- "I never stick with anything."
- "There's no point starting again."

Then practice a different script:

- "I paused. Now I'm continuing."
- "Today is still worth showing up for."
- "I can restart without starting over."

Simply turn to the next page and begin again. Your Must life is not cancelled by interruptions; it is shaped by what you do after them.

Using the book with others

Though your answers are personal, you do not have to walk this path alone. You might:

- Read the same day as a partner or friend and discuss your reflections.
- Use selected days as conversation starters in a small group.
- Share occasional questions (not every private page) with a coach, counselor, or spiritual director.

If you do this, remember: your words here are yours. Share only what feels safe and meaningful to share.

At milestones and year's end

Scattered through the year are days that ask you to look back—at the last week, month, or quarter; at what changed; at what life seems to be trying to teach you.

Do not skip those. They:

- Show you progress you would otherwise miss.
- Keep you from treating every struggle as a fresh failure.
- Turn experience into usable wisdom instead of just memory.

By the time you reach the final pages, you will have walked through a full "year in review," written in your own hand. You will be invited to close this chapter not with a tidy bow, but with a clear sense of who you are becoming next.

One last guideline

If you remember nothing else about how to use this book, remember this:

You are not here to perform. You are here to tell yourself the truth and treat that truth with respect.

Do that, one page at a time, and the *Must Year* will have done its work.

THE MUST CIRCLE OF LIFE

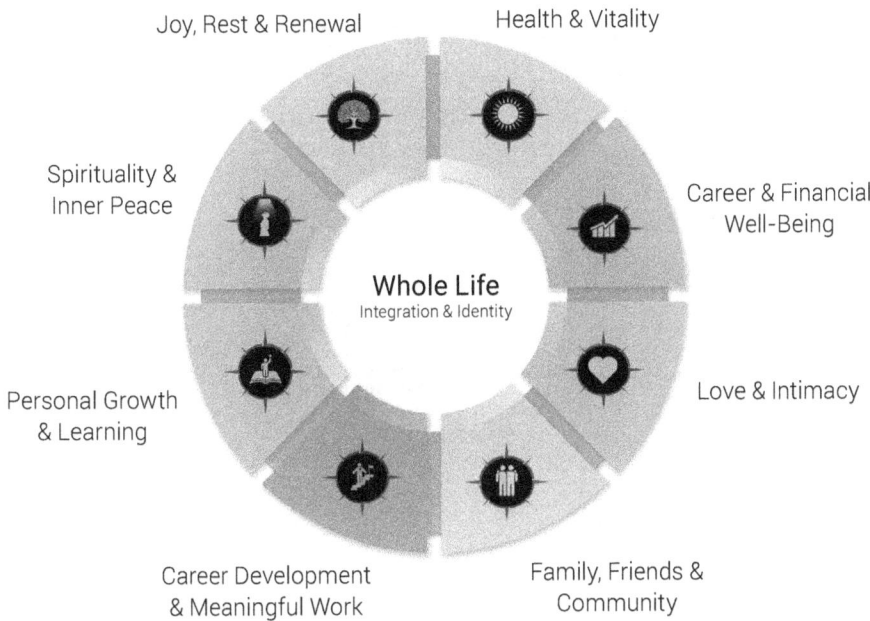

A Whole-Life Map for Reflection, Strength, and Daily Alignment

The **Must Circle of Life** is your visual guide to the major domains that shape a flourishing life.

Earlier Must work centers on seven core domains. *Must Year* expands that circle with two additional lenses—Joy, Rest & Renewal and Whole Life Integration—to support a more complete, emotionally grounded year of becoming.

You can use this Circle in several ways:

As a quick snapshot of your current life—where you feel strong, where you feel stretched, and where you feel neglected.

As a reminder that no single domain has to carry everything for long; your year will move through all of them in a steady rhythm.

To notice patterns over time, especially when one area repeatedly asks for more honesty or care.

Joy, Rest & Renewal and Whole Life Integration are highlighted in *Must Year* to deepen your daily experience. Together, they help you design not only a productive year, but a more balanced, vibrant, and coherent life.

MY BEGINNING IDENTITY STATEMENT

My Must Statement – Beginning

This page is for you to name, as honestly as you can today, the kind of person you are choosing to become.

Do not worry about perfect words. You're not locking anything in; you're choosing a direction.

You might begin with:

- "I am someone who is meant to…"
- "I am becoming a person who…"
- "My life is a Must when I…"

Take your time. When you are ready, write your statement below and add today's date.

Date: _____

My current Must identity statement is:

_____

_____

_____

_____

(You may return to this page later and adjust your words. For now, let it be a snapshot of who you are choosing to be at the start of this *Must Year.*)

WAKING UP TO YOUR LIFE

Becoming Awake to Yourself (Days 1–90)

The first quarter and season of your *Must Year* is about waking up to the life you are actually living. Before you can change anything with integrity, you need to see clearly your patterns, your energy, your relationships, your work, your money, your faith, your rest, and the stories you tell yourself about all of it.

Across Days 1–90, you will rotate through every domain of your life. You will notice what feels alive and what feels numb, what is working and what is quietly draining you, where you feel proud and where you feel stuck. The goal of this season is not to fix everything at once, but to tell the truth about where you are and begin listening to the person you are becoming.

As you move through Season 1, let your main questions be:

- "What is really here?"
- "What have I been pretending not to notice?"
- "What might be trying to change in me?"

By the time you reach the Season 1 Marker, you will have a more honest picture of your current life—and a clearer sense of what your Must self is asking you to pay attention to next.

DAY 1

Health & Vitality × Story

You've been telling a story about your body for so long that it started to feel factual. "This is just how I am." "I never stick with it." "I'll get serious later." Those quiet sentences decide what you reach for, how late you stay up, and how quickly you quit when change moves slower than your hope.

But your body is not a verdict—it's a relationship. It remembers the seasons you abandoned and the ones when you returned. A *Must Year* isn't about becoming perfect; it's about shifting the story from "I failed again" to "I came back again." Every small choice is either repeating an old chapter or quietly beginning a new one.

Today's Must Reflection

Where did you repeat an old story about your body—about your general health, energy, how you look or feel in your body, age, or discipline—and if you answered as the person you're becoming instead, how would that sentence change?

DAY 2

Career & Financial Well-Being × Beliefs

You learned what was "too much," "selfish," or "impossible" from people who were doing the best they could, often while carrying their own fear and very real constraints.

If you still spend, save, or stay small from their fear alone, you're still living by someone else's fears. A Must life honors what you were taught and what you're up against but refuses to let yesterday's panic be the only voice shaping tomorrow's possibilities. You are allowed to believe your work matters, your contribution carries value, and your life deserves more than bare survival—even if circumstances are tight right now.

Today's Must Reflection

What belief about money or work did you inherit that no longer fits the person you're becoming—and what truer, more realistic belief are you willing to try on, even if it feels uncomfortable at first?

DAY 3

Love & Intimacy × Self Image

Love isn't just about who you choose; it's also about who you believe you are when someone chooses you. If deep down you see yourself as "too much," "not enough," or permanently wounded, you apologize for who you are, even when you don't need to.

The problem isn't that you're unlovable; it's that you've rehearsed an image of yourself that you can't receive love without suspicion. A *Must Year* urges you to try seeing yourself through a truer lens —to see yourself as someone capable of learning, worthy of kindness, and allowed to be imperfect without forfeiting intimacy.

Today's Must Reflection

When you're with the person you love (or hope to love), who do you secretly believe you are—and what one small action could you take today as if you were already worthy of uncomplicated, steady love?

DAY 4

Family, Friends & Community × Environment

You didn't choose the first table you sat at in life. You were born into rooms already loud with opinions, expectations, and unfinished stories. Your family and early friendships sketched outlines of who you were allowed to be.

Now you're old enough to ask a harder question: does your current circle reflect your Must life or your maintenance life? Your environment always shapes you—one way or the other. The people closest to you either keep you playing small or quietly insist that you rise. Choosing air that lets you breathe is not betrayal—it's responsibility.

Today's Must Reflection

If your current relationships formed a room you had to live in for a year, what in that room gives you oxygen—and what quietly pulls it away?

DAY 5

Career Development & Meaningful Work × Vision

Purpose rarely arrives as a job title. It usually begins as a restlessness you can't fully explain. You feel it when a conversation wakes something in you, when an injustice makes you burn, or when you lose track of time doing something that doesn't yet "fit" on a résumé.

The mistake is waiting for permission or clarity before you move. Vision rarely appears in high definition. It begins as a direction, not a map. A *Must Year* asks you to trust the small next step, not the idealized future version. Purpose often reveals itself while your feet are already in motion.

Today's Must Reflection

Where in your life do you keep saying, "One day I'll…"—and what is the smallest visible step in that direction you could take within the next 24 hours?

DAY 6

Personal Growth & Learning × Self-Talk

The words you whisper to yourself in quiet moments shape more of your life than the words you say out loud. Self-talk doesn't shout; it quietly shapes your life. A single sentence—"I can't," "I always mess this up," "This is just who I am"—can turn a doorway into a wall.

A *Must Year* is not about perfect positivity. It's about honest self-respect. It's speaking to yourself the way you would speak to someone you love who is learning how to rise. Your self-talk sets the weather inside your mind. Today, choose a climate that allows something new to grow.

Today's Must Reflection

What phrase do you repeat to yourself that limits who you're becoming—and what would a more honest, respectful sentence be instead?

DAY 7

Spirituality & Inner Peace × Stillness

Stillness isn't about everything around you going quiet—it's about you becoming attentive to what is happening within. You can be standing in a crowded room or racing through a busy day and still feel deeply anchored when your inner world is steady. Peace has far less to do with the noise around you and far more to do with the posture you hold inside.

A *Must Year* reminds you that stillness is strength. Slowness is not weakness; silence is not emptiness. When you lower the noise, what remains is clarity—the kind that doesn't shout but always tells the truth.

Today's Must Reflection

Where in your life do you feel the most noise—and what is one small way you can create a pocket of stillness today?

DAY 8

Joy, Rest & Renewal × Rest Patterns

You can't pour from a cup you refuse to refill. Yet many people treat rest as a reward for exhaustion rather than a requirement for a meaningful life. Your patterns around rest often come from what you saw growing up—who was allowed to pause, who had to push through, and what it meant to be "strong."

A *Must Year* reframes rest as responsibility. Renewal isn't indulgence; it's maintenance of your capacity to love, work, think, and show up with integrity. Rest is not what you do when everything is done—it's what allows you to do everything well.

Today's Must Reflection

What rest pattern have you been repeating that drains you—and what would a healthier pattern look like today?

DAY 9

Health & Vitality × Energy Leaks

Your energy is one of the most honest storytellers in your life. It reveals the conversations that drain you, the habits that dull you, the tasks that matter, and the ones that only pretend to. When your energy leaks, it's not a moral failure—it's feedback.

A *Must Year* gently suggests you treat energy as information, not judgment. Pay attention to what pulls you down and what builds you up. Energy doesn't lie. If you follow it, it will tell you exactly where your boundaries, alignment, and next steps need to be.

Today's Must Reflection

Where did your energy dip this week—and what was the truth that moment was trying to tell you?

DAY 10

Whole Life Integration × Check-In

Ten days may not feel like much, but patterns reveal themselves quickly when you're paying attention. A Whole-Life Check-In is a moment to zoom out and see the shape of your days: where you felt aligned, where you drifted, and what surprised you.

This isn't about judgment; it's about awareness. When you look at the last ten days honestly, you can see the beginning of a story—one you're either continuing unconsciously or choosing to shape with intention. Small shifts now make big changes inevitable later.

Today's Must Reflection

Looking back over the last ten days, what pattern are you beginning to notice—and what's one shift you want to carry into the next ten?

DAY 11

Career & Financial Well-Being × Alignment

Work drains you most when it requires you to shrink. Even if the job looks impressive on paper, misalignment feels like grit in your gears. You push harder, stay later, say yes when you mean no—but your spirit pays the interest. Alignment isn't about finding the perfect job; it's about refusing to abandon the parts of you that know the truth.

A *Must Year* asks you to notice where your work life feels honest and where it feels borrowed. The goal isn't immediate change. The goal is seeing clearly. When you name misalignment, you stop calling exhaustion "normal."

Today's Must Reflection

Where in your work or financial life are you acting in ways that don't match your values—and what small, doable step would bring more alignment this week?

DAY 12

Love & Intimacy × Receiving

It's easier to give love than to receive it. Receiving requires you to believe you are worthy without performing, proving, or earning. It asks you to unclench the parts of yourself that learned to survive by staying separate or endlessly helpful. Receiving love is an act of trust: trust in another person and trust in who you are becoming.

A *Must Year* whispers to you to notice when love feels unfamiliar. Instead of turning away from it, let it sit beside you. Your capacity to receive is part of your healing—and part of your becoming.

Today's Must Reflection

When someone offers you love, care, or kindness, what do you typically do—and what would it look like to receive it without shrinking?

DAY 13

Family, Friends & Community × Belonging

Belonging isn't about shrinking yourself to match the room—it's about standing as who you truly are and feeling received rather than tolerated. You don't earn belonging by blending in; you experience it when truth is met with acceptance. Time alone doesn't create that kind of connection—shared courage and shared honesty do.

A *Must Year* nudges you to question where you feel seen and where you feel edited. You deserve relationships where your presence isn't tolerated but welcomed. Belonging is less about finding the right people and more about recognizing the places where your soul can exhale.

Today's Must Reflection

Where in your life do you feel true belonging—and where do you feel the need to perform or hide?

DAY 14

Career Development & Meaningful Work × Curiosity

Curiosity is the doorway to purpose. You don't have to know your five-year plan; you only need to follow the small sparks that make you wonder, question, or lean forward. We often dismiss curiosity because it feels too subtle, too soft, too impractical—but most callings begin as a gentle pull, not a grand announcement.

A *Must Year* encourages you to take your curiosity seriously. It is one of the few honest signals your life gives you. Where there is sustained curiosity, there is often direction.

Today's Must Reflection

What topic, idea, or activity has been quietly pulling your attention—and what tiny step could you take to explore it?

DAY 15

Personal Growth & Learning × Identity

Identity is not fixed; it is shaped by what you repeatedly say "yes" or "no" to. The person you think you are is often just the person you've practiced being. When you change the practice, you change the identity. You do not become someone new—you uncover the parts of you that were waiting for permission to emerge.

A *Must Year* helps you notice the small choices that reinforce who you're becoming. Each choice is a brushstroke on the portrait of your future self. Paint with intention.

Today's Must Reflection

What choice did you make recently that felt aligned with the person you want to become—and how can you repeat that alignment today?

DAY 16

Spirituality & Inner Peace × Surrender

Surrender is not giving up; it is giving over. It's the moment you stop forcing what your spirit knows is not yours to carry. Surrender is clarity wrapped in humility—the willingness to release what you cannot control so you can finally hold what is meant for you.

A *Must Year* pushes you to stop wrestling with every burden and to trust that release is its own kind of wisdom. Some things change the moment you stop gripping them. Some paths open only when your hands are free.

Today's Must Reflection

What are you holding tightly out of fear—and what would it feel like to loosen your grip, even a little, today?

DAY 17

Joy, Rest & Renewal × Joy Memory

Inside you lives a memory of joy that never fully disappeared. It may be faint, buried beneath responsibilities or worn down by years of being "the strong one," but it's still there—waiting. Joy is not childish or irresponsible; it is fuel. It reminds you that your life is more than the tasks you complete or the roles you fulfill.

A *Must Year* asks you to return to the moments that made your spirit feel light, expansive, and alive. Joy is not a luxury. It is evidence that you are still connected to something true.

Today's Must Reflection

What is one small moment from your past that made you feel real joy—and how could you recreate even a small piece of that today?

DAY 18

Health & Vitality × Listening

Your body speaks in whispers long before it ever raises its voice. The trouble is that we ignore the whispers—fatigue, tension, irritability—until they become symptoms we can no longer outrun. Listening to your body is not self-indulgence; it is wisdom.

A *Must Year* teaches you to treat your body as a partner, not an obstacle. When you listen early, you don't have to recover later. Your body has been trying to tell you something. Today, let yourself hear it.

Today's Must Reflection

What physical or emotional signal has your body been giving you lately—and what is the simplest way you can respond with care?

If this reflection brings up intense or overwhelming feelings, consider talking with a qualified mental health or medical professional; you do not have to carry this alone.

DAY 19

Whole Life Integration × Pattern

Patterns are your life's quiet architecture. They shape your days long before you consciously choose them. If you look closely, you'll see that most frustrations you experience today echo frustrations from years ago—not because life repeats, but because patterns do.

A *Must Year* asks you to look at your life through the lens of pattern rather than circumstance. Patterns tell the truth faster than stories do. Once you see a pattern clearly, you can finally decide whether to continue it—or rewrite it.

Today's Must Reflection

What repeating pattern has shown up again this week—and what truth is it revealing about your choices or needs?

DAY 20

Career & Financial Well-Being × Self-Worth

Your work mirrors what you believe you're worth. Not your salary—your sense of value. If deep down you think your needs are "too much" or your voice is inconvenient, you will settle for roles that shrink you or pay you in praise instead of progress. Your work rises to the level of your self-worth.

A *Must Year* helps you confront the places where you've traded authenticity for approval. When you honor your worth, you stop chasing scraps. You start creating opportunities that align with the truth of who you are.

Today's Must Reflection

Where have you been accepting less than you deserve in your work or financial life—and what boundary or honest conversation would honor your worth?

DAY 21

Career Development & Meaningful Work × Beliefs

Most people carry a private belief about why they are here, even if they rarely say it out loud. It might be "to help," "to build," "to create," or "to protect." Over time, that belief can get buried under bills, routines, or the weight of other people's expectations.

A *Must Year* implores you to stop treating that belief as a distant dream and start seeing it as a signal. You don't need the full picture to respect the pull. You only need to admit that something in you keeps pointing in the same direction for a reason.

Today's Must Reflection

What simple statement about why you are here keeps returning to you—and what is one small choice this week that agrees with that belief instead of ignoring it?

DAY 22

Personal Growth & Learning × Self Image

Change often starts on the inside before anyone else can recognize it. You may think differently, notice your patterns sooner, or feel uncomfortable in situations that used to feel normal. Your inner life evolves faster than your outer life can catch up.

This tension doesn't mean you're pretending; it means you're in transition. A *Must Year* helps you respect the person you're becoming even while you still live inside yesterday's routines. That respect shows in the way you speak to yourself—and in what you choose next.

Today's Must Reflection

Where do you already feel different on the inside, even if nothing external has changed yet—and what is one visible action that would support that new version of you?

DAY 23

Spirituality & Inner Peace × Emotions

Many people learn that certain emotions don't belong in spiritual settings—anger, doubt, disappointment, confusion. So, they try to tidy themselves up before they pray, reflect, or step into any space they consider sacred.

Pushing feelings down doesn't make them disappear; it splits you in two. Inner peace grows when you stop editing yourself and start bringing your real inner life to the table. A *Must Year* encourages you to believe that your emotions aren't a problem to hide—they're part of the truth that needs to be seen.

Today's Must Reflection

Which emotion do you usually keep out of your spiritual life—and what is one safe way you could be more honest about that feeling (in writing, in prayer, or with someone you trust)?

DAY 24

Joy, Rest & Renewal × Vision

Your week may be filled with responsibilities, checklists, and endless movement—but almost empty of simple enjoyment and rest. Over time, that emptiness becomes numbness, resentment, or quiet burnout.

Joy and rest aren't luxuries; they're part of a steady, sustainable life. In a *Must Year*, you treat enjoyment and recovery as essential inputs, not rare rewards. Even small shifts can restore your energy, patience, and clarity.

Today's Must Reflection

If you were to make your week just a little more livable, what small, specific activity could you add—a walk, a hobby, a moment of rest—and when will you do it?

DAY 25

Health & Vitality × Environment

Your environment either supports your health or quietly works against it. When your space is dark, cluttered, or dominated by screens, it becomes much easier to stay up late, overeat, or slip into inactivity. A more intentional space makes the better choice feel natural instead of forced.

You don't have to redo your entire home. One or two small adjustments—placing water where you see it, creating a calm corner, or moving your phone out of reach at night—can send a message to your body that change has begun.

Today's Must Reflection

Look at the place where you usually start or end your day. What is one practical change you could make there that would help your body feel more cared for?

DAY 26

Career & Financial Well-Being × Emotions

Money decisions often look logical on the surface but are driven by emotions underneath—fear, guilt, shame, pride, or hope. When you focus only on the numbers, you repeat the same patterns without understanding why.

In a *Must Year*, you don't judge yourself for how you've handled money or work. Instead, you get curious. You ask, "What was I feeling when I did that?" Once you recognize the emotion, you gain the power to choose differently next time.

Today's Must Reflection

Think of one recent money or work decision you're not fully happy with. What feeling was driving it—and what feeling would you prefer to guide your next choice?

DAY 27

Love & Intimacy × Habits

Strong relationships are built on consistent, simple actions—not just big conversations. A sincere message, a thoughtful question, or a few minutes of undistracted presence can matter more than long speeches or grand gestures.

When life gets busy, these small acts are the first to disappear. A *Must Year* helps you answer a powerful question: "What does love look like in ordinary time?" Then you translate that answer into habits you can keep.

Today's Must Reflection

What small, repeatable way can you show care to someone who matters to you—a brief check-in, a note, a call—and how will you build it into your day?

DAY 28

Family, Friends & Community × Vision

Think of the people you want beside you ten years from now. Imagine how you want it to feel when you're together—warm, honest, steady, safe enough to be real.

Those future moments will be shaped by how you show up today. You can't control anyone else's growth, but you can choose to become someone who is easier to be honest with and safer to be close to. A *Must Year* helps you cultivate that kind of presence with intention.

Today's Must Reflection

Choose one person you hope to stay close to long term. How would you like them to describe what it feels like to be around you—and what is one step you can take toward that description?

DAY 29

Career Development & Meaningful Work × Story

There's the story you tell others about your work, and there's the story you tell yourself when you're alone. The public story might focus on practicality, stability, or obligation. The private story often holds questions about meaning, fit, or desire.

Ignoring the private story doesn't make it disappear; it just makes you feel off center. A *Must Year* compassionately suggests to you to bring that inner story into the light—not to make drastic decisions, but to see clearly. Honest awareness is the first step toward alignment.

Today's Must Reflection

If you wrote two brief descriptions of your work life—"what I say" and "what I really feel"—how would they differ, and what truth in the second one needs your attention?

DAY 30

Whole Life × Integration

Thirty days can feel both fast and slow. On one hand, you may think, "Not much has changed." On the other, you might notice subtle shifts—new thoughts, better questions, clearer boundaries, or moments of awareness that didn't exist before.

Those small shifts are the foundation of transformation. A *Must Year* isn't about instant change; it's about consistent direction. When you keep turning toward who you're meant to be, the outer changes eventually follow.

Today's Must Reflection

Looking back over these first thirty days, where do you notice even a small shift in how you think, feel, or act—and what intention do you want to carry into the next thirty?

DAY 31

Health & Vitality × Habits

Most people wait for a burst of motivation before changing their health. But motivation fades quickly. What truly changes your body, your energy, and your confidence are the small things you repeat when you are *not* motivated.

A *Must Year* focuses on identity-based habits: "I am someone who takes care of my body," not "I am someone trying to fix myself." When you act from that identity—even in tiny ways—you build trust in yourself. Small repetitions create a life you can rely on.

Today's Must Reflection

What is one very small, repeatable action a person who cares for their body would do today—and when exactly will you do it?

DAY 32

Career & Financial Well-Being × Identity

It's easy to say, "I'm bad with money," or "I'm stuck in my career." Those identity statements feel true only because they've been repeated—not because they are permanent.

Every time you handle money thoughtfully or take one meaningful step in your work, **you reinforce the identity you are growing into**—someone capable with finances, steady under pressure, or willing to rise after difficulty.

Today's Must Reflection

Finish this sentence honestly: "I see myself as someone who _____ with money/career." What is one small action today that would slightly upgrade that sentence?

DAY 33

Love & Intimacy × Communication

Arguments often go in circles because each person is defending a position instead of revealing a need. "You never listen" really means "I need to feel heard." "You're too demanding" really means "I need to feel free and respected."

In a *Must Year*, you practice speaking from the need instead of the accusation. That one shift can lower the temperature of a conversation and open a new way forward.

Today's Must Reflection

Think of a recent tension with someone you care about. If you stripped away the complaint, what need was underneath—and how could you express that need more clearly?

DAY 34

Family, Friends & Community × Boundaries

Being kind and being endlessly available are not the same thing. When you say yes while your whole body is saying no, you may preserve peace on the surface while quietly building resentment underneath.

Healthy boundaries are not walls; they are doors with working handles. They let in what nourishes you and limit what drains you. In a *Must Year*, your "no" becomes a way of telling the truth—not a sign that you love people less.

Today's Must Reflection

Where in your relationships have you been saying yes when you honestly want to say no—and what is one clear, respectful boundary you could set or reinforce?

DAY 35

Career Development & Meaningful Work × Small Experiments

Many people try to discover their purpose only in their minds. They analyze, overthink, and worry—but rarely test anything in real life. But clarity comes from movement, not just thought.

A *Must Year* encourages "small experiments"—teaching one class, volunteering once, starting one tiny project. These experiments give you real feedback: energy, boredom, curiosity, resistance, joy. Over time, the pattern becomes undeniable.

Today's Must Reflection

What is one low-risk, small experiment you could run in the next week that might teach you something about your purpose or calling?

DAY 36

Personal Growth & Learning × Self Honesty

Growth often begins with a simple, difficult sentence: "This isn't working anymore." It might apply to how you eat, how you work, how you relate, or how you talk to yourself. Admitting the truth feels scary because it raises the question, "So what now?"

In a *Must Year*, you don't shame yourself for the past. You simply let the truth be clear enough to act on. Self-honesty isn't an attack; it's an opportunity for growth.

Today's Must Reflection

Where in your life do you quietly know, "This isn't working for me anymore"—and what is one honest step you could take in response?

DAY 37

Spirituality & Inner Peace × Daily Practice

A powerful insight can feel transformative, but without practice it fades. What steadies you over time is a simple, repeatable way of turning your attention inward or upward—something you can do on ordinary days, not just extraordinary ones.

This practice doesn't need to be long or dramatic. It might be a short prayer, a few breaths, a quiet reading, or a moment of pause before work. In a *Must Year*, the point isn't to perform—it's to be present.

Today's Must Reflection

What small, realistic daily practice could you add—or return to—that helps you feel more grounded and connected, and when will you do it today?

DAY 38

Joy, Rest & Renewal × Guilt

Many people feel guilty when they rest or experience joy—especially when others are struggling or when their to-do list is long. That guilt drains the power of rest and steals the nourishment joy is meant to bring.

The truth is that rest is part of your responsibility. A burned-out version of you cannot give your best gifts or make your clearest decisions. In a *Must Year*, rest becomes part of your service, not the opposite of it.

Today's Must Reflection

When you think about resting or doing something enjoyable, what guilty thought shows up—and what more truthful thought could you choose instead?

DAY 39

Health & Vitality × Self-Talk

Your body absorbs the tone of the way you speak about it. Harsh, shaming self-talk might feel like it will push you to change, but it usually creates more discouragement, tension, and giving up. Honest, respectful self-talk doesn't pretend everything is fine—it helps you face what's hard in a way that supports real change.

In a *Must Year*, you experiment with speaking to yourself the way you'd speak to a close friend who wants to change their life—honest but kind, direct but hopeful.

Today's Must Reflection

What is one harsh sentence you often think or say about your body or energy—and how could you rewrite it to be both truthful and respectful?

If this reflection brings up intense or overwhelming feelings, consider talking with a qualified mental health or medical professional; you do not have to carry this alone.

DAY 40

Career & Financial Well-Being × Long View

Short-term pressure can make money and career choices feel urgent and reactive. You grab what's in front of you or avoid making decisions at all. But when you zoom out and think in terms of years instead of days, new options appear.

A *Must Year* urges you to ask, "What would my future self thank me for?" That single question can shift how you handle debt, savings, skills, time, and opportunities. You're not just managing today—you're building the life your future self will have to live with.

Today's Must Reflection

If you imagined yourself five years from now, what is one money or career decision you could make this month that your future self would be grateful for?

DAY 41

Love & Intimacy × Boundaries

In close relationships, silence can feel easier than honesty. You swallow the comment that stung, take on more than you have capacity for, or stay quiet to avoid conflict. Over time, that silence builds distance inside you—even when you remain physically close.

Healthy love includes limits. Boundaries are not punishments; they are protections for the relationship and for your well-being. In a *Must Year*, you practice saying, "This works for me, and this does not," with clarity, respect, and courage.

Today's Must Reflection

Think of a recent moment in a close relationship when you felt overrun or resentful. What boundary would have helped—and what is one small way you can express it now?

DAY 42

Family, Friends & Community × Expectations

Every relationship carries unspoken expectations—how often you talk, how quickly you reply, what you share, how available you are. When these expectations don't match, people feel hurt, confused, or overlooked, often without understanding why.

A *Must Year* suggests you notice your own expectations and communicate them openly. You also begin asking others what they expect instead of guessing. This simple step prevents misunderstandings that quietly erode connection.

Today's Must Reflection

Choose one important relationship. What do you silently expect from this person—and what do you think they silently expect from you?

DAY 43

Career Development & Meaningful Work × Values

Purpose is not only in what you do—it's in the values your work expresses. Two people can have the same job, yet one treats it as a transaction while the other approaches it as a chance to practice service, creativity, compassion, excellence, or growth.

When you connect your daily tasks to your core values, even ordinary work begins to matter. In a *Must Year*, you ask, "How can I bring what matters most to me into what I am already doing?"

Today's Must Reflection

Identify one core value that matters deeply to you. How could you express that value more clearly through the work or responsibilities you already have?

DAY 44

Personal Growth & Learning × Identity

Who you believe yourself to be shapes what you attempt. If you quietly think, "I always fail," or "I can't change," you will unconsciously act in ways that reinforce that belief. Identity statements are powerful—even when they're inaccurate.

In a *Must Year*, you begin telling a different story: "I am learning." "I am growing." "I am someone who tries again." You do not pretend to be finished; you simply commit to becoming.

Today's Must Reflection

Write a supportive identity statement (e.g., "I am someone who follows through," or "I am someone who faces what matters"). What is one action you can take today that aligns with that new identity?

DAY 45

Spirituality & Inner Peace × Connection

Many people feel alone even when surrounded by others. They move through their days on autopilot, disconnected from anything larger than their routines or responsibilities. Over time, life begins to feel flat and joyless.

Inner peace grows when you remember your place in something bigger—a faith, a community, a tradition, a purpose, or simply the shared human experience of trying and growing. A *Must Year* encourages you to pause and reconnect with that larger story.

Today's Must Reflection

When was the last time you felt genuinely connected to something bigger than yourself—and what is one simple way you could invite that feeling back?

DAY 46

Joy, Rest & Renewal × Intention

When you're younger, joy happens naturally. As life fills with obligations, if you don't make space for enjoyment, it quietly disappears. You look up and realize weeks have passed without a single moment that felt light, creative, or restorative.

Intentional joy doesn't mean forced positivity. It means planning small, genuine activities that refill you—without needing to be productive, impressive, or shared online. In a *Must Year*, you give joy a place on your calendar, not just in your imagination.

Today's Must Reflection

What simple activity reliably makes you feel more alive—and when in the next seven days will you make space for it?

DAY 47

Health & Vitality × Awareness

Before you change anything about your health, you must first see it clearly. Many people rush, scroll, snack, or stay up late without noticing the patterns. They just feel "off" and blame themselves in vague ways.

Awareness is not judgment—it's information. In a *Must Year*, you gently ask: When am I most tired? When do I reach for comfort? When do I feel grounded? This noticing gives you specific places to begin.

Today's Must Reflection

Without judgment, what is one health-related pattern you've noticed this week—around sleep, food, movement, or stress—and what might that pattern be trying to give you?

DAY 48

Career & Financial Well-Being × Learning

Money and career decisions feel overwhelming when you assume you should already know everything. That pressure can paralyze you. But you don't need expertise to begin—you only need curiosity.

In a *Must Year*, you treat money and work as skills you can grow into. You read, ask questions, take a small class, or talk to someone further along. Each bit of learning reduces fear and expands your choices.

Today's Must Reflection

What is one thing about money or career you wish you understood better—and what is one small step you could take this week to learn about it?

DAY 49

Love & Intimacy × Self-Respect

The way you allow others to treat you often mirrors the way you treat yourself. If you dismiss your own needs, ignore your feelings, or tolerate behaviors that diminish you, others may start unconsciously doing the same.

Self-respect is not harshness; it's honoring your worth in daily practice. In a *Must Year*, you match your standards for relationships with the way you care for yourself.

Today's Must Reflection

In what small, everyday way could you show yourself more respect—and how might that shift what you accept from others?

DAY 50

Family, Friends & Community × Appreciation

It's easy to focus on what's missing—the conversations you wish you'd had, the support you didn't receive, the misunderstandings still lingering. Those experiences are real. But focusing only on gaps can freeze connection.

Appreciation doesn't erase the hard parts; it simply rounds out the truth. Naming what you value in someone often encourages more of that behavior and softens your heart at the same time. In a *Must Year*, you practice saying what you usually only think.

Today's Must Reflection

Choose one person in your life. What is one specific thing you genuinely appreciate about who they are or what they've done—and how could you express it to them soon?

DAY 51

Health & Vitality × Priorities

There is always more you *could* do for your health—more steps, more water, more sleep, more appointments. But when everything becomes a priority, nothing truly changes.

In a *Must Year,* you choose one focus at a time. Maybe this month it's sleep. Maybe it's daily movement. Maybe it's reducing one habit that leaves you drained. Clarity creates momentum.

Today's Must Reflection

If you had to choose *one* health priority for the next 30 days, what would it be—and what is one simple first step toward it?

DAY 52

Career & Financial Well-Being × Work–Life Balance

When work consumes most of your energy, everything else eventually weakens—your relationships, health, creativity, and rest. Yet if you neglect your work and finances, stress follows you into every part of your life.

Balance doesn't mean equal time; it means giving the right things the right attention so nothing essential collapses. In a *Must Year*, you regularly ask, "What needs more of me right now—and what needs less?"

Today's Must Reflection

Looking at this week, which area—work, health, relationships, or rest—needs more of your attention, and where might you gently pull back?

DAY 53

Love & Intimacy × Listening

Feeling loved often comes less from perfect words and more from feeling heard. When you listen only to respond, people feel managed. When you listen to understand, they feel safe.

In a *Must Year*, you slow down your reactions. You let the other person finish. You check that you understood. It won't solve everything, but it can change how conversations feel.

Today's Must Reflection

In your closest relationship, how often do you truly listen without planning your response—and what is one small way you could listen more fully?

DAY 54

Career Development & Meaningful Work × Courage

Sometimes you already know the next step toward a more authentic life—and still avoid it. Not because it's unclear, but because it's frightening. What if you fail? What if you look foolish? What if someone is disappointed?

Courage isn't about eliminating fear; it's choosing to move anyway, even with your heart trembling. In a *Must Year*, you don't wait to feel fearless. You aim to be slightly braver than your fear for a few minutes at a time.

Today's Must Reflection

What is one step you already know you need to take toward a more authentic life—and what fear has been holding you back?

DAY 55

Love & Intimacy × Emotional Availability

Many relationships struggle not because of a lack of love, but because of a lack of emotional availability. You may care deeply for someone and still stay guarded—answering with facts instead of feelings, humor instead of honesty, or silence instead of vulnerability.

These protections were learned for a reason. They kept you safe when openness wasn't safe. But in a healthy relationship, guardedness becomes distance. You cannot be fully loved if you are only partially present.

A *Must Year* helps you practice opening the door a little wider—not by oversharing or forcing intimacy, but by letting someone see one honest feeling at a time. Emotional availability is less about saying everything and more about letting yourself be seen.

Today's Must Reflection

When someone you care for asks how you're doing, what part of your inner world do you usually hold back—and what is one small, safe way you could share a little more today?

DAY 56

Personal Growth & Learning × Reflection

Life moves quickly. Without reflection, you can repeat the same month twelve times and call it a year. Reflection slows you down long enough to notice patterns, lessons, and quiet wins you might otherwise miss.

In a *Must Year*, reflection isn't overthinking—it's asking a few meaningful questions regularly: What worked? What hurt? What helped? What do I want more or less?

Today's Must Reflection

Looking back at the last week, what is one thing that went well, one thing that was hard, and one thing you'd like to try differently next week?

DAY 57

Spirituality & Inner Peace × Self-Compassion

Many people speak to themselves more harshly than they ever would to a friend. When they make a mistake, they attack instead of support. Over time, this inner cruelty makes peace difficult to find.

Self-compassion is not excusing everything; it's choosing to respond to your own struggles with truth and care rather than shame. In a *Must Year*, you practice speaking to yourself the way a wise and kind mentor would.

Today's Must Reflection

Think of something you're disappointed about in yourself right now. If a close friend had done the same thing, what would you say to them—and how can you offer some of that same grace to yourself?

DAY 58

Joy, Rest & Renewal × Simple Pleasures

You may be waiting for a big trip, a major celebration, or "someday" to finally enjoy life. Meanwhile, ordinary days pass with very little that feels pleasant or light.

Often, simple pleasures—good coffee, a favorite song, a short walk, a warm conversation—do more for your daily mood than rare, spectacular experiences. In a *Must Year*, you intentionally plant these small joys into your ordinary days.

Today's Must Reflection

What low-effort, simple pleasure could you include today—a sensory experience, a brief connection, or a small treat—and when will you do it?

DAY 59

Health & Vitality × Stress

Stress isn't only what happens to you; it's how you respond on the inside Two people can face similar pressures yet experience very different levels of strain, depending on their beliefs, habits, and coping strategies.

In a *Must Year*, you don't deny stress. Instead, you ask, "What helps me come back down?" You identify specific actions—breathing, walking, reaching out, writing—that reduce tension rather than numb it.

Today's Must Reflection

When you feel stressed, what do you usually do—and what is one healthier way of releasing stress that you could try next time it builds?

DAY 60

Career & Financial Well-Being × Identity Review

After sixty days of small steps, it can be easy to overlook something important: these actions are shaping who you believe yourself to be. You may already feel more like someone who chooses, not just reacts.

Identity changes through repeated behaviors, not dramatic moments. In a *Must Year*, reflection is not judgment—it's recognition. Even imperfect effort is evidence of a new kind of person emerging.

Today's Must Reflection

Complete this sentence about yourself today: "*I am becoming someone who...*"

What words fit honestly based on the last sixty days?

DAY 61

Love & Intimacy × Trust

Trust grows slowly and breaks quickly. It is built through small, consistent choices: keeping your word, telling the truth even when it's uncomfortable, repairing instead of defending, and handling emotions with steadiness rather than volatility.

In a *Must Year*, you shift your attention from *wanting trust* to *becoming trustworthy*—in how you handle secrets, time, promises, and your own reactions.

Today's Must Reflection

In your closest relationship, what is one specific way you could be more trustworthy this week?

DAY 62

Family, Friends & Community × Time

Most people say their relationships matter most—yet give them whatever time is left after work, social media time, and exhaustion. Over months and years, that "leftover" time shapes your sense of connection or distance.

In a *Must Year*, you do not wait for a perfect free day. You intentionally protect small pockets of time: a call, a walk, a shared meal, an unhurried conversation. Small consistency strengthens bonds.

Today's Must Reflection

Who is one person you care about but haven't given enough focused time to lately—and what is one simple way you could connect with them soon?

DAY 63

Career Development & Meaningful Work × Strengths

Purpose often hides inside what feels natural to you. Because something feels easy, you may dismiss it as unimportant. Yet your strengths are often the places where you contribute most effortlessly and joyfully.

In a *Must Year*, you take your strengths seriously. You notice when others thank you, seek your help, or say, "You're really good at that." These moments reveal abilities that may deserve more space in your life and work.

Today's Must Reflection

What is something people often compliment you on or ask for your help with—and how might that ability play a larger role in a meaningful life?

DAY 64

Personal Growth & Learning × Discomfort

Growth almost never arrives dressed as ease. New patterns feel clumsy at first. Honest conversations can shake your confidence. Changing long-held habits can leave you feeling unsteady. But uneasiness is not a sign you've taken a wrong turn—it's the natural sensation of becoming someone new.

In a *Must Year*, you learn to distinguish between the discomfort of *stretching* and the pain of *self-betrayal*. One moves you toward who you're becoming; the other pulls you away.

Today's Must Reflection

Where in your life are you feeling discomfort right now—and does it feel more like stretching or going against yourself?

If this reflection brings up intense or overwhelming feelings, consider talking with a qualified mental health or medical professional; you do not have to carry this alone.

DAY 65

Spirituality & Inner Peace × Gratitude

The mind naturally searches for what's missing or wrong. Over time, this can make a good life feel inadequate, even when there is much to appreciate. Gratitude doesn't erase struggles; it broadens your vision.

In a *Must Year*, gratitude becomes a practice, not a personality trait. You train your attention to notice small, specific moments of goodness, steadiness, or kindness—even on difficult days.

Today's Must Reflection

List three specific things from the last 24 hours you are genuinely grateful for—and what each one offered you.

DAY 66

Joy, Rest, & Renewal × Creativity

Creativity is not limited to artists; it is the everyday act of making something new—new solutions, new connections, new forms of expression, new ways of enjoying life. It awakens parts of you that routine keeps quiet.

In a *Must Year*, you welcome small creative moments back into your days: a new recipe, a rearranged room, a written paragraph, a rough sketch, a small idea captured. These simple acts restore your inner spark.

Today's Must Reflection

What is one small creative act you could do today—not to impress anyone, but to awaken your own curiosity?

DAY 67

Health & Vitality × Boundaries with Technology

Screens are woven into modern life, but without boundaries they quietly erode your sleep, mood, focus, and relationships. You may realize you check your phone more often than you check in with yourself.

In a *Must Year*, you treat technology as a tool—not a master. Simple limits such as "no phone at meals," a nighttime cutoff, or focused work blocks can dramatically protect your energy and presence.

Today's Must Reflection

What is one realistic boundary you could set with your phone or screens this week that would help your mind and body rest?

DAY 68

Career & Financial Well-Being × Satisfaction

You can be busy and still feel empty. You can also be in a simple role and feel deeply satisfied. Satisfaction often comes down to two questions: *Does what I do matter to me?* and *Am I growing?*

In a *Must Year*, you do not ignore dissatisfaction. You listen to it. It may be asking for new challenges, clearer meaning, healthier boundaries, or an entirely different direction.

Today's Must Reflection

On a scale from 1–10, how satisfied are you with your work or primary role—and what is one thing that would move that number up by one point?

DAY 69

Love & Intimacy × Apologies

A real apology is more than "I'm sorry." It includes understanding, ownership, and a willingness to change: "I see how that hurt you. I did that. I want to do better."

Without this level of repair, old hurts stack up and trust erodes. With it, intimacy deepens.

In a *Must Year*, you learn to repair sooner—without excuses, minimization, or defensiveness. Humility strengthens connection.

Today's Must Reflection

Is there someone you owe a clearer apology to—and what would you need to acknowledge for it to be honest and complete?

DAY 70

Family, Friends & Community × Honest Self-Expression

You may hide parts of yourself—your interests, beliefs, doubts, or hopes—because you fear conflict or judgment. Over time, this hiding creates emotional distance, even when you see someone regularly.

In a *Must Year*, you practice bringing a bit more of your true self into the relationships that matter. Not all at once, and not with everyone, but enough that you stop disappearing inside your own life.

Today's Must Reflection

Where do you feel you can't fully be yourself with people you care about—and what is one small truth that feels safe enough to share?

DAY 71

Health & Vitality × Motivation

Motivation rises and falls. Some days you feel ready to overhaul everything; other days you can barely manage the essentials. If you only act on the energized days, progress becomes inconsistent and discouraging.

In a *Must Year*, you build routines that work even when motivation is low—simple, repeatable actions that are small enough for hard days yet meaningful enough to move you forward on good ones.

Today's Must Reflection

What is one health-related action that feels realistic even on a tired or stressful day—and when will you do it today?

DAY 72

Career & Financial Well-Being × Clarity

Vague desires—"be successful," "make more money," "do meaningful work"—give your brain nothing to aim at. Clear goals provide direction, reduce anxiety, and help you recognize real opportunities.

In a *Must Year*, you define what "better" specifically means for you: a type of role, a skill level, a savings amount, a schedule, a team culture, or a kind of daily impact. With clarity, the next step becomes obvious.

Today's Must Reflection

In one sentence, describe a work or money situation that would feel "better" to you one year from now.

DAY 73

Love & Intimacy × Emotional Safety

Closeness requires emotional safety—the sense that you can be honest without being mocked, dismissed, or punished. Without safety, people withdraw, perform, or become careful versions of themselves.

In a *Must Year*, you notice how it feels to share your inner world and how safe others feel around you. You work toward responses that make honesty easier, gentler, and more welcome.

Today's Must Reflection

With someone important to you, do you feel safe being honest about your feelings—and do they likely feel safe being honest with you? Why or why not?

DAY 74

Family, Friends & Community × Old Patterns

Long-standing relationships often run on old patterns—who apologizes first, who avoids conflict, who fixes everything, who gets loud, who shuts down. These roles can follow you into adulthood even when they no longer fit.

In a *Must Year*, you notice when you slip into an old role and gently ask, "Is this how I want to show up now?" Awareness alone begins to shift the pattern.

Today's Must Reflection

What is one recurring pattern you fall into with family or long-time friends—and what would a healthier response look like?

DAY 75

Career Development & Meaningful Work × Joy Signals

Purpose often shows up as quiet joy—the deep, steady feeling that something "fits." You may sense it when you lose track of time, feel useful, or experience a blend of challenge and satisfaction.

In a *Must Year*, these joy signals become data. You pay attention to what consistently energizes you—activities, conversations, problems you enjoy solving, ways you naturally help.

Today's Must Reflection

Think of a recent moment when you felt genuinely engaged and alive. What were you doing, and what part of it felt so right?

DAY 76

Personal Growth & Learning × Feedback

Feedback can sting, especially when delivered poorly. Yet sometimes even awkward or uncomfortable feedback contains a piece of truth that could help you grow.

In a *Must Year*, you separate *how* something was said from *what* might be useful. You keep what supports your future self and release what doesn't.

Today's Must Reflection

Recall a piece of feedback—recent or old—that bothered you. Is there any small part of it that could help you if you used it wisely?

DAY 77

Spirituality & Inner Peace × Alignment

Inner peace comes from alignment—living in a way that matches your deepest values. When your behaviors drift far from what you say matters, internal tension grows.

In a *Must Year*, you regularly ask, "Does my time, attention, and effort reflect what I truly care about?" You don't fix everything at once—you make small, continuous adjustments back toward alignment.

Today's Must Reflection

Name one value that matters deeply to you. Where in your weekly life is that value clearly visible—and where is it missing?

DAY 78

Joy, Rest, & Renewal × Social Pressure

Many people try to have fun the way others do—drinking when they don't want to, staying out when they're exhausted, or forcing activities that leave them drained rather than restored.

In a *Must Year*, you redefine fun and rest on your own terms. You ask, "What actually leaves me feeling better afterward?" and give yourself permission to choose that, even if it looks different from what others prefer.

Today's Must Reflection

What is something others seem to enjoy that doesn't truly work for you—and what is an alternative that genuinely restores you?

DAY 79

Health & Vitality × Identity

If you see yourself as "the unhealthy one," "the tired one," or "the one who never sticks with it," you will often behave in ways that confirm that belief. Identity quietly shapes action.

In a *Must Year*, you adopt a new identity: "I am someone who is learning to care for my body." Small, consistent actions begin to reinforce that truth, even if you still feel like a beginner.

Today's Must Reflection

Write a new identity sentence about your health (for example, "I am someone who honors my energy"). What is one small action today that aligns with that identity?

DAY 80

Career & Financial Well-Being × Progress Check

Comparison makes you feel behind, even when you're moving forward. But real progress in work and money is often slow, personal, and uneven.

In a *Must Year*, you measure progress by *your* steps—skills developed, fears faced, habits improved, conversations initiated, small financial gains made. You let evidence, not comparison, define growth.

Today's Must Reflection

Over the last few months, what is one clear sign that you've moved forward in work or finances, even if you're not where you ultimately want to be?

DAY 81

Health & Vitality × Wellness Definition

"Being healthy" can mean very different things depending on your season of life. For some, it's strength and stamina. For others, it's calm, restorative sleep, or simply being able to move without pain.

In a *Must Year*, you define wellness on your own terms instead of chasing vague or inherited standards. When you clarify what "well" looks and feels like to you, the right choices become clearer and more compassionate.

Today's Must Reflection

In your own words, what does "being well" mean for you right now—and how is that different from what you used to believe?

If this reflection brings up intense or overwhelming feelings, consider talking with a qualified mental health or medical professional; you do not have to carry this alone.

DAY 82

Career & Financial Well-Being × "Enough"

Without a personal sense of "enough," more is never enough—more income, more recognition, more work. But when you define what "enough" means for you, a surprising sense of peace and focus appears.

In a *Must Year*, you ask grounded questions: What is enough to feel secure? What is enough to feel purposeful? What is enough to feel balanced? Your answers evolve as you do, but clarity begins the shift.

Today's Must Reflection

If you were to describe "enough" in your finances or work in one or two sentences, what would you say?

DAY 83

Love & Intimacy × Love Definition

People use the word "love" without ever naming what it truly means to them. Is it presence? Loyalty? Kindness? Honesty? Support? Your definition shapes what you accept—and what you give.

In a *Must Year*, you become more specific. Clarity helps you recognize genuine love and notice when something called "love" isn't aligned with your deepest values.

Today's Must Reflection

Complete the sentence: "To me, love means…" What stands out in your answer?

DAY 84

Family, Friends & Community × Roles

In groups, people often slip into familiar roles—the helper, the peacemaker, the planner, the comedian, the quiet one. These roles may have once served you but can eventually confine you.

In a *Must Year*, you notice which role you automatically inhabit and ask whether it still reflects who you are becoming. You're allowed to outgrow old labels.

Today's Must Reflection

What role do you usually play in your family or friend group—and what part of yourself gets left out when you stay in that role?

DAY 85

Career Development & Meaningful Work × "Want"

You may be skilled at sensing what others want from you—but far less practiced at asking what *you* want. Over time, ignoring your own desires leads to numbness, resentment, or a sense of living someone else's life.

In a *Must Year*, "What do I want?" becomes a legitimate and necessary question. Honest answers illuminate your path—not selfishness.

Today's Must Reflection

If no one would be disappointed and nothing bad happened, what is one change you secretly want to make in your work or direction?

DAY 86

Personal Growth & Learning × Self-Knowledge

Growth is not just about fixing weaknesses; it is also about understanding how you actually operate—your triggers, patterns, strengths, fears, and limits.

In a *Must Year*, everyday situations become mirrors. Instead of thinking "I messed up again," you ask, "What did this show me about myself?" This shift turns mistakes into clarity instead of shame.

Today's Must Reflection

Think of a recent situation that didn't go as you hoped. What did your reaction reveal about your needs, fears, or habits?

DAY 87

Spirituality & Inner Peace × Questions

Spiritual life is often portrayed as answers. But for many people, it begins with better questions: "What matters most?" "What kind of person am I becoming?" "What do I believe about love, forgiveness, meaning?"

In a *Must Year*, you allow those questions to sit without rushing to cover them with clichés. Honest questions expand your spiritual depth and ground you in sincerity.

Today's Must Reflection

What is one honest question about life, meaning, or faith you've been carrying—and what would it look like to sit with it instead of forcing an answer?

DAY 88

Joy, Rest, & Renewal × Balance

Too much "fun" that leaves you depleted—late nights, overstimulation, constant noise—doesn't feel like rest. But too much rigid rest with no joy leaves life flat and dull.

In a *Must Year*, you find a balance: activities that feel good *and* leave you better afterward. This kind of nourishment supports your whole life instead of draining it.

Today's Must Reflection

Think of something you do to "relax" that actually leaves you more tired. What is one alternative that would leave you calmer or more refreshed?

DAY 89

Health & Vitality × Mental Health

Your mind and body are deeply interconnected. Exhaustion, tension, and poor sleep affect mood. And emotional strain—anxiety, sadness, unprocessed grief—often shows up physically.

In a *Must Year*, you honor both. You don't dismiss emotional struggles as "just in your head," and you don't ignore the physical habits that could support your mind.

Today's Must Reflection

Right now, does your mind feel more tired or your body more tired—and what is one gentle action that would help the more exhausted part?

If this reflection brings up intense or overwhelming feelings, consider talking with a qualified mental health or medical professional; you do not have to carry this alone.

DAY 90

Career & Financial Well-Being × Whole-Life Impact

Career and financial choices ripple through your entire life. A job that looks good on paper but drains your energy, relationships, and health carries a hidden cost. A simpler role that preserves well-being may be worth far more.

In a *Must Year*, you ask bigger questions: "How will this decision affect my whole life—my peace, health, time, relationships, and spirit?" This broader lens leads to wiser, more sustainable choices.

Today's Must Reflection

Think of one career or money decision you're considering. How might it affect your health, relationships, and inner life—not just your finances?

Quarter 1 – Waking Up to Your Life

You have completed the first quarter of your *Must Year*.

These early days have asked you to do something most people avoid: look at your real life with clear eyes. You have explored how you treat your body, your money, your time, your close relationships, your work, your faith, and your rest. You have noticed patterns and stories you once took for granted.

The first quarter is about **awareness and honesty**. Before you can build a Must life, you must see the life you are actually living.

Take a moment to look back over Days 1–90. Skim your answers. Notice:

- Where you wrote more.
- Where you resisted.
- Where certain themes repeat.

You are not judging; you are observing.

Season 1 Reflection

You may want to answer these on a blank page nearby:

1. Over these first 90 days, what three themes or issues showed up most often in your writing?
2. Which life domains (health, money, love, family, purpose, growth, spirituality, fun) felt most tender or activated?
3. Where did you surprise yourself—with honesty, with clarity, or with something you admitted for the first time?

4. What is one old script about yourself you have started to question?
5. If you chose a quiet intention for the next 90 days, based on what you see here, what would it be?

As you move into Quarter 2, you will begin to work more deliberately with boundaries, experiments, and new identity statements. The point is not to "fix everything," but to respond to what you have now seen.

You are more awake to your life than you were three months ago. That is the work of this quarter.

SEASON 2

PRACTICING NEW WAYS OF BEING

Experiments, Boundaries & Small Bravery (Days 91–180)

This season is about embodiment. You begin living the truths you uncovered in Quarter 1—not perfectly, but consistently. Patterns start to shift, choices sharpen, and your inner world becomes steadier and more intentional.

Quarter 2 is where growth becomes movement. You practice letting go of what drains you and strengthening what aligns with your identity. You build rhythms that honor who you are becoming. You begin to live from your Must in small, repeated acts of courage throughout your days.

You're entering Quarter 2 — Practicing New Ways of Being

DAY 91

Love & Intimacy × Receiving

For many people, giving feels natural while receiving feels uncomfortable. Accepting help, affection, or praise can trigger vulnerability, as if receiving makes you weak, dependent, or indebted.

In a *Must Year*, you practice letting love land. Receiving is not selfish—it is part of genuine connection. It tells the other person their care matters and that you value the relationship.

Today's Must Reflection

When someone offers kindness, help, or affirmation, how do you usually respond—and what would it look like to receive it just a little more openly?

DAY 92

Family, Friends & Community × Conflict

Conflict is unavoidable anywhere people care about each other. Avoiding every hard conversation may keep things quiet on the surface, but underneath, resentment and misunderstanding quietly grow. Distance forms not because you fought, but because you never told the truth.

In a *Must Year*, conflict is not proof that a relationship is broken; it is an invitation to clarity. Speaking honestly---with respect and humility---gives the relationship a chance to grow stronger and more honest than before. Silence might feel safer, but it also keeps you stuck in guesses rather than real understanding.

Today's Must Reflection

Think of a conflict you've been avoiding. What is the one truth you need to express—and what would be a respectful way to begin that conversation?

DAY 93

Career Development & Meaningful Work × Contribution

Purpose is not limited to large, public accomplishments. It is also found in small, steady acts of contribution—encouraging someone, solving a problem, creating calm, or bringing clarity where there was confusion.

In a *Must Year*, you look for the places where your presence quietly makes things better. These moments reveal how you naturally serve the world around you.

Today's Must Reflection

Where in your current life—home, work, or community—do you already make things better for others, even in small ways?

DAY 94

Personal Growth & Learning × Self Talk in Failure

When something goes wrong, your inner voice can either help you grow or shut you down. "I failed; I'm done" closes the door. "I failed; what can I adjust?" keeps the door open.

In a *Must Year*, you treat failures as feedback. You still feel disappointment, but you also ask, "What is this teaching me about my next step?"

Today's Must Reflection

Recall a recent setback. If you viewed it purely as information, what would it be telling you to change, try, or prepare for?

DAY 95

Spirituality & Inner Peace × Practices That Don't Fit

You may have tried spiritual or reflective practices that never felt natural—rituals, routines, or traditions that left you feeling more distant than grounded. It's easy to assume the problem is you.

In a *Must Year*, you give yourself permission to experiment. The right practice is the one that helps you be more honest, compassionate, and connected—not simply the one you were taught to imitate.

Today's Must Reflection

Is there a spiritual or reflective practice you've kept doing out of obligation, even though it doesn't help—and what might be a more honest, helpful alternative?

DAY 96

Joy, Rest, & Renewal × Solo vs. Social

Some people recharge alone; others refill through connection. Many need a blend of the two. If you only rest one way, you may never get what your mind and body truly need.

In a *Must Year*, you pay attention to what kind of rest you've been missing—quiet solitude, easy company, or genuine play—and you adjust intentionally.

Today's Must Reflection

Do you feel more restored after time alone or time with others—and what kind of rest have you been missing lately?

DAY 97

Health & Vitality × Medical Support

There are moments when "trying harder" is not enough. Persistent pain, overwhelming fatigue, or emotional heaviness may signal something deeper—something that deserves professional attention.

In a *Must Year*, seeking help is an act of courage and wisdom. You honor your life by inviting the right experts into your care.

Today's Must Reflection

Is there a physical or mental health concern you've been minimizing or postponing—and what is one concrete step you could take to address it?

If this reflection brings up intense or overwhelming feelings, consider talking with a qualified mental health or medical professional; you do not have to carry this alone.

DAY 98

Career & Financial Well-Being × Integrity

Career or financial success can come at the cost of integrity—cutting corners, staying quiet when something feels wrong, or choosing status over substance. Over time, these choices wear down your self-respect.

In a *Must Year*, integrity becomes part of how you define success. You aim for achievements that allow you to feel proud of how you earned them.

Today's Must Reflection

Where in your work or financial life do you feel a pull between what is easy and what is right—and what small step would move you closer to integrity?

DAY 99

Love & Intimacy × Knowing Yourself

Healthy relationships require self-awareness. Without it, you may over-accommodate, suppress your needs, or suddenly withdraw when unspoken feelings build up.

In a *Must Year*, you treat knowing yourself as foundational to loving others well. The clearer you are about your needs, triggers, and boundaries, the kinder and more consistent you can be.

Today's Must Reflection

What is one personal need—emotional, physical, or relational—that often appears in your relationships, and how could you express it more clearly?

DAY 100

Family, Friends & Community × Milestones

Relationships move through seasons—beginnings, conflicts, reconciliations, transitions, losses, and deepening. Acknowledging these milestones helps you see how far you've come together and how the story is evolving.

In a *Must Year*, you take a moment to notice and honor these turning points instead of rushing past them. Recognition strengthens connection.

Today's Must Reflection

Choose one relationship that has changed over the last few years. What milestone—big or small—could you quietly honor or acknowledge?

DAY 101

Health & Vitality × Control vs. Acceptance

Some aspects of your health are within your influence—movement, sleep routines, nutrition, stress tools. Others—genetics, past injuries, chronic conditions, unexpected illness—are not.

In a *Must Year*, you separate what you can shape from what you cannot. This frees your energy for meaningful action and softens your frustration around what is truly beyond your control.

Today's Must Reflection

In your health right now, what is one thing you *can* influence—and one thing you clearly cannot?

DAY 102

Career & Financial Well-Being × Daily Experience

It is easy to evaluate work only by title, salary, or reputation and ignore the lived experience of your daily life. But your actual day—the pace, people, tasks, and environment—shapes your well-being far more than any label.

In a *Must Year*, you pay attention to how work *feels*, not just how it appears. You notice what energizes you, what drains you, and what feels neutral. This awareness becomes a compass for wiser choices.

Today's Must Reflection

If you described a typical workday in three words, what would they be—and how close are those words to how you'd *like* your days to feel?

DAY 103

Love & Intimacy × Attachment

Everyone has patterns in how they attach—how quickly they open, how they react to distance, how they handle fear of loss. Some move closer, some pull away, some toggle between both depending on stress.

In a *Must Year*, you approach your attachment style with curiosity rather than criticism. Understanding your pattern helps you explain yourself to partners and shift how you respond when you feel triggered.

Today's Must Reflection

When you feel insecure in a close relationship, do you tend to move *toward* the other person, *away* from them, or go numb—and what does that usually look like?

DAY 104

Family, Friends & Community × Seasons

Not every relationship is meant to stay the same forever. Some are for a season, some for a purpose, some for the long haul. Holding tightly to every connection can keep you from accepting healthy, natural change.

In a *Must Year*, you honor the role people have played in your story while allowing relationships to shift—closer, looser, or sometimes to end with compassion.

Today's Must Reflection

Is there a relationship that may have fit a past season but no longer fits the same way now—and what honest shift might be needed?

DAY 105

Career Development & Meaningful Work × Legacy

"Legacy" can sound grand, but its simplest meaning is this: what remains of you when you're not in the room. Your legacy is being shaped right now through small interactions—how you listen, help, lead, or speak.

In a *Must Year,* you ask, "If someone described the impact I've had on them, what would I hope they'd say?" That vision becomes a guide for how you show up today.

Today's Must Reflection

If one person in your life described your impact in a single sentence, what would you *hope* they'd say—and what could you do today that supports that?

DAY 106

Personal Growth & Learning × Limiting Beliefs

Limiting beliefs often disguise themselves as facts: "I'm not disciplined." "People like me can't do that." "It's too late for someone my age." Left unchallenged, they quietly shrink your life.

In a *Must Year*, you begin catching these beliefs and asking, "Is this absolutely true—and who gains from me believing it?" Even the smallest doubt about a limiting belief creates room for new behavior.

Today's Must Reflection

What is one long-standing belief about yourself or your potential that may be limiting you—and what evidence, even small, challenges it?

DAY 107

Spirituality & Inner Peace × Everyday Moments

Spirituality or deep meaning is not limited to sacred spaces or special rituals. It often shows up in ordinary moments: sunlight on the floor, a quiet drive, washing dishes, a breath before a meeting, a gentle thought.

In a *Must Year*, you begin treating daily life as fertile ground for presence, gratitude, and honesty—not just formal "spiritual" practices.

Today's Must Reflection

What is one everyday moment where you could pause for a few seconds and bring a sense of presence, gratitude, or awareness?

DAY 108

Joy, Rest, & Renewal × "Should" vs. "Want"

You may fill your free time with what you think you *should* do—catching up on tasks, consuming content, or saying yes to invitations that drain you—instead of what genuinely restores you.

In a *Must Year*, you ask, "What do I truly want or need right now?" And you let at least part of your downtime reflect that answer.

Today's Must Reflection

In your next block of free time, what would you choose if you set aside the "shoulds" and listened to what you actually want?

DAY 109

Health & Vitality × Morning or Evening Anchor

Days become easier to navigate when you have a steady point—a simple morning or evening ritual that gives your mind and body a sense of rhythm.

In a *Must Year*, you explore one small anchor habit: a short walk, a stretch, a devotional reading, a moment of reflection, or a few quiet breaths at the same time each day.

Today's Must Reflection

Would a morning anchor or evening anchor help you more right now—and what small, 5–10 minute practice could serve as that anchor?

DAY 110

Career & Financial Well-Being × Productivity vs. Meaning

You can be highly productive—checking boxes, meeting deadlines—yet feel disconnected from meaning. Productivity answers "How much did I do?"; meaning answers "Why did it matter?"

In a *Must Year*, you aim to weave both together. You honor your responsibilities, but you also look for the connection between your work and your deeper values.

Today's Must Reflection

Looking at the past few days, which task or interaction felt most meaningful—and what made it meaningful to you?

DAY 111

Love & Intimacy × Shared Vision

Strong relationships depend not only on how you feel today but also on the direction you're walking together. If your long-term visions diverge sharply, tension eventually appears—even when the present feels good.

In a *Must Year*, you talk not only about logistics and problems, but also about dreams, values, plans, and desires. You look for overlap—and you pay attention to places where alignment is missing.

Today's Must Reflection

With someone you're close to, do you have a clear sense of what you both want in the long run—and where does it feel aligned or misaligned?

DAY 112

Family, Friends & Community × Emotional Labor

In many relationships, one person quietly carries most of the emotional load: remembering, checking in, smoothing conflicts, interpreting moods, or maintaining closeness. Over time, this imbalance becomes exhausting.

In a *Must Year*, you notice how much emotional labor you give—and how much you allow yourself to receive. Healthy connection shares this work more evenly.

Today's Must Reflection

In one meaningful relationship, do you carry most of the emotional labor, or do they—and what small shift would make it feel more balanced?

DAY 113

Career Development & Meaningful Work × "If Not Now, When?"

There is always a reason to wait—money, timing, confidence, age, approval. Some delays are wise; others are fear disguised as practicality.

In a *Must Year*, you respect real constraints but ask a bracing question: "If I don't begin moving toward this now, when realistically will I?" That honesty breaks long cycles of waiting.

Today's Must Reflection

What is one change or project you've been delaying for more than a year—and what is the honest reason you haven't started?

DAY 114

Personal Growth & Learning × Curiosity

When something goes wrong, many people default to blame—of themselves or others. Blame anchors you to the past. Curiosity opens the door to change: "What led to this?" "What was I feeling?" "What could shift next time?"

In a *Must Year*, you replace "What's wrong with me/them?" with "What's happening here?" That small shift lowers shame and increases insight.

Today's Must Reflection

Think of a recurring problem in your life. If you approached it with curiosity instead of blame, what new question would you ask about it?

DAY 115

Spirituality & Inner Peace × Forgiveness of Self

You may carry past regrets like a private weight—things you said, choices you made, seasons you wish you could redo. Holding on can feel responsible, but it often keeps you stuck in the past.

In a *Must Year*, forgiving yourself doesn't mean pretending the moment didn't matter. It means deciding that it doesn't get to define your entire identity or future. You take the lesson and release the self-punishment.

Today's Must Reflection

What is one past decision you still punish yourself for—and what would it mean to say, "I was human. I learned. I'm allowed to move forward"?

DAY 116

Joy, Rest, & Renewal × Playfulness

Playfulness is not childish—it is the ability to be light, curious, and unguarded for a moment. Without play, life becomes heavy even when nothing is "wrong."

In a *Must Year*, you invite harmless silliness back into your days: joking, trying something new poorly, doing something simply because it's fun. This flexibility strengthens your resilience in more serious parts of life.

Today's Must Reflection

When was the last time you did something purely for fun, without worrying how it looked—and what small playful act could you try this week?

DAY 117

Health & Vitality × Food Relationship

Food is never just food. It carries emotion, memory, comfort, restraint, identity, and sometimes conflict. Strict rules or total chaos around eating can both signal a strained relationship with food.

In a *Must Year*, you move gently toward a kinder, more balanced approach—one where you respect your body's needs, enjoy eating, and notice when emotions rather than hunger drive your choices.

Today's Must Reflection

Think of a recent time you ate when you weren't physically hungry. What were you actually needing or feeling in that moment?

DAY 118

Career & Financial Well-Being × Networking

"Networking" can sound shallow or transactional, but at its best, it is simply building genuine relationships—exchanging ideas, sharing opportunities, and learning from people you respect.

In a *Must Year*, you approach networking not as collecting contacts but as connecting with real human beings in your field who inspire you. A few honest relationships matter more than many superficial ones.

Today's Must Reflection

Who is one person you respect in your field whom you could reach out to in a simple, genuine way?

DAY 119

Love & Intimacy × Appreciation vs. Fixing

In close relationships, it's easy to focus on what you want someone to change and forget to notice what you truly appreciate. Constant fixing can make a partner feel like a project—not a person.

In a *Must Year*, you aim to name what's good at least as often as what needs improvement. Appreciation creates safety, strengthens connection, and makes hard conversations easier.

Today's Must Reflection

Think of someone you love. What is one specific behavior or quality you genuinely appreciate but rarely say out loud?

DAY 120

Family, Friends & Community × Belonging

Belonging is more than being welcomed; it is being able to show your full self without fear of losing connection. Some relationships offer conditional belonging—you are accepted only as long as you stay within certain lines.

In a *Must Year*, you notice where you feel free and where you feel you must shrink or perform. This clarity guides where you invest your limited relational energy.

Today's Must Reflection

Where in your life do you feel the strongest sense of "I can be myself here"—and where do you feel you must hide parts of who you are?

DAY 121

Health & Vitality × Pace

Your body has a natural pace. When you constantly override it—too many commitments, not enough recovery—it eventually pushes back through fatigue, irritability, or illness.

In a *Must Year*, you begin noticing when your daily rhythm runs faster than your body can sustainably handle. Instead of waiting for a forced stop, you experiment with small adjustments that honor your limits.

Today's Must Reflection

If your body could set the pace today, what is one thing it would ask you to slow down on—or remove entirely?

DAY 122

Career & Financial Well-Being × Comparison

Comparing your career or finances to others almost always leaves out crucial context—different histories, opportunities, constraints, and values. Comparison frequently produces unnecessary shame or inflated pride.

In a *Must Year*, you use others' stories for inspiration, not measurement. Your true progress is measured against your own starting point, situation, and goals.

Today's Must Reflection

Where do you most often compare yourself in work or finances—and what is a healthier, more personal standard you could use instead?

DAY 123

Love & Intimacy × Boundaries with Self

Boundaries aren't only about others—they're also about how you treat yourself. You may cross your own boundaries through overworking, self-criticism, or staying in situations that consistently harm you.

In a *Must Year*, you draw a line by saying, "I will no longer treat myself this way." This includes stopping behaviors that erode your dignity and choosing those that honor your worth.

Today's Must Reflection

What is one way you regularly cross your own boundary—and what is one small step toward changing that pattern?

DAY 124

Family, Friends & Community × Listening to History

Everyone carries a history—family patterns, cultural shaping, trauma, success—that influences how they show up now. Forgetting this can make you take things too personally or oversimplify their behavior.

In a *Must Year*, you remember that people's reactions often say as much about their past as about the present moment. This awareness doesn't excuse harm but can soften your response and bring clarity.

Today's Must Reflection

Think of someone whose behavior frustrates or confuses you. What part of their history might help explain—though not justify—how they show up?

DAY 125

Career Development & Meaningful Work × Saying No

Every "yes" costs something—time, energy, focus. When you say yes automatically, you may crowd out the space required for meaningful work or needed rest.

In a *Must Year*, saying "no" becomes part of your purpose. You decline what clearly does not support who you are becoming, even when it would be easier to agree.

Today's Must Reflection

What current commitment does not support the life you're building—and what would it look like to renegotiate or release it?

DAY 126

Personal Growth & Learning × Identity Upgrades

Deep change often occurs through small, steady "identity upgrades"—shifting from "I never do this" to "I sometimes do this" to "I'm becoming someone who does this regularly."

In a *Must Year*, you pay attention when your actions begin to match your future self more than your old self. Those moments gently reshape your identity.

Today's Must Reflection

Think of a recent moment where you handled something differently than the "old you" would have. What does that say about who you're becoming?

DAY 127

Spirituality & Inner Peace × Boundaries with Input

What you consume—news, social media, conversations, media—shapes your inner world. Regular exposure to outrage or comparison slowly drains peace and clarity.

In a *Must Year*, you set gentle boundaries around what enters your mind and spirit. You choose inputs that inform, and uplift more than they agitate or exhaust.

Today's Must Reflection

Is there a source of input (feed, show, site, or person) that consistently leaves you anxious or angry—and what boundary could you set with it?

DAY 128

Joy, Rest & Renewal × Unstructured Time

If every moment is scheduled, your nervous system never fully exhales. Unstructured time—without a plan or task—can feel unfamiliar, but it gives your mind space to wander, settle, and reset.

In a *Must Year*, you leave small pockets of time open on purpose. Not filling every gap becomes an act of care.

Today's Must Reflection

When was the last time you had an hour with no plan and no screen—and what small window of unstructured time could you create this week?

DAY 129

Health & Vitality × Identity Around Age

Beliefs about age—"too old," "too young," "that ship has sailed"—shape behavior more than actual ability. Many of these beliefs are cultural, not biological.

In a *Must Year*, you treat age as context, not limitation: "Given my season, what remains possible, wise, and exciting?" Often, the answer is far more than you assumed.

Today's Must Reflection

What is something you've told yourself you're "too old" or "too young" for—and is that truly a fact, or mostly a story?

DAY 130

Career & Financial Well-Being × Identity as Provider

Seeing yourself as "the provider"—financially, emotionally, or otherwise—can be meaningful but heavy. This identity may drive you to over-function and quietly neglect your own needs.

In a *Must Year*, you value your role without letting it erase your humanity. Being a provider does not mean never needing rest, support, or care.

Today's Must Reflection

In what ways do you see yourself as a provider—and where might you need to allow others to support you as well?

DAY 131

Love & Intimacy × Routine vs. Intention

Relationships often slide into routine—same conversations, same patterns, same touch points. Routine can feel safe, but without intention it slowly dulls connection.

In a *Must Year*, you pause to ask, "Are we just repeating, or are we relating?" Small intentional choices—a thoughtful question, a genuine compliment, a shared activity—can reopen connection where autopilot has settled in.

Today's Must Reflection

What is one small, intentional action you could take this week to break routine and invite real connection?

DAY 132

Family, Friends & Community × Honoring Differences

People you love may think, cope, or believe differently than you do. Forcing sameness usually increases tension; honoring real differences reduces it.

In a *Must Year*, you practice respectful disagreement. You allow others to take their path while setting boundaries that protect your peace. Unity doesn't require uniformity.

Today's Must Reflection

Where in your relationships do you struggle most with accepting differences—and what would "respect without agreement" look like there?

DAY 133

Career Development & Meaningful Work × Tiny Consistency

Big purpose is often built on small, repeated actions—writing a paragraph, learning a skill, making a call, practicing ten minutes. The size of the action matters less than if it happens consistently.

In a *Must Year*, you choose a tiny, nearly fail-proof practice that keeps you connected to meaningful work even on busy days. Consistency becomes your ally.

Today's Must Reflection

What is one extremely small daily action that would keep you close to your purpose—and how can you make it almost impossible to skip?

DAY 134

Personal Growth & Learning × Owning Your Part

In conflict, it is easy to catalog someone else's mistakes and harder to acknowledge your own. Yet repair often begins with recognizing your contribution—what you said, assumed, escalated, or ignored.

In a *Must Year*, you do not take on blame that isn't yours, but you do own your part clearly. This strengthens character and softens defensiveness.

Today's Must Reflection

Think of a recent tension. What is one specific thing you said or did that you could have handled better?

DAY 135

Spirituality & Inner Peace × Values in Action

Values matter most when lived. Compassion, honesty, humility, and forgiveness hold meaning only when expressed in real choices, especially during hard moments.

In a *Must Year*, you choose one value and practice it visibly—through tone, decisions, and how you respond to stress. Living your values brings inner steadiness.

Today's Must Reflection

Pick one value you associate with your spiritual or moral life. What is one concrete way you could practice it today?

DAY 136

Joy, Rest & Renewal × Permission

You may wait for an external signal to rest, slow down, or enjoy yourself. That permission may never come.

In a *Must Year*, you begin giving yourself permission based on what you need—not what circumstances dictate. Rest becomes a responsible choice, not an indulgence.

Today's Must Reflection

If you granted yourself full permission to rest or enjoy one simple thing today, what would you choose?

DAY 137

Health & Vitality × Self-Monitoring

Your body gives early cues—tension, cravings, fatigue, irritability—that something needs attention. Ignoring these signs often leads to larger problems later.

In a *Must Year*, you check in with yourself regularly. You treat these signals as useful information, not interruptions.

Today's Must Reflection

Right now, what is your body communicating through its energy, tension, or cravings—and what might it be asking for?

DAY 138

Career & Financial Well-Being × Skill Building

Feeling stuck often comes from relying on the same skills you've always had. New skills—technical, relational, creative—unlock new paths and possibilities.

In a *Must Year*, you treat skill building as an investment in your future self. Even small steps can create opportunities you cannot yet see.

Today's Must Reflection

What is one skill that, if improved even slightly, would help your work or financial life—and what is a realistic first step?

DAY 139

Love & Intimacy × Check-Ins

Cars and homes get routine maintenance—relationships need it too. Regular check-ins allow small issues to surface before they become deep cracks.

In a *Must Year*, you ask open questions and listen without defensiveness. Honest check-ins are not signs of trouble; they are signs of care.

Today's Must Reflection

With someone close to you, what is one honest question you could ask this week about how they're feeling in the relationship?

DAY 140

Family, Friends & Community × Letting People Be Themselves

You can exhaust yourself trying to change people who don't want to change. Giving advice they didn't request, pushing growth they're not ready for, carrying responsibility they won't shoulder—it drains both sides.

In a *Must Year*, you allow people to be who they are while adjusting your distance or expectations. You focus your energy on what *you* can change.

Today's Must Reflection

Who in your life are you tired of trying to "fix"—and what boundary or shift in expectations would honor both them and you?

DAY 141

Career Development & Meaningful Work × Environment

Your surroundings can either support or suffocate your sense of purpose. A cluttered or chaotic space makes it harder to think clearly about what matters; an intentional space reminds you of who you're becoming.

In a *Must Year*, you don't wait for a perfect office. You carve out even a small corner—a chair, a desk, a notebook—that signals, "Here is where I honor what matters."

Today's Must Reflection

What is one small change you could make to your environment that would better support the work or calling you care about?

DAY 142

Personal Growth & Learning × Patience

Understanding usually comes before transformation. You may grasp something mentally long before your habits fully match your insight. Impatience can make you quit just as the new pattern is forming.

In a *Must Year*, you embrace the truth that progress is uneven—two steps forward, one step back. You measure direction, not perfection.

Today's Must Reflection

Where are you being too hard on yourself for "not changing fast enough"—and what would a more patient, long-view perspective sound like?

DAY 143

Spirituality & Inner Peace × Silence

Stillness can feel strange at first if you're used to constant noise. Yet quiet moments are often where you finally hear what's happening inside—and sometimes, what you sense beyond yourself.

In a *Must Year*, you experiment with pockets of silence. Not to force an experience, but to give your mind a moment to settle and reset.

Today's Must Reflection

When was the last time you sat in real silence for even a few minutes—and what might you notice if you tried it today?

DAY 144

Joy, Rest & Renewal × Nature

Modern life keeps you indoors, often in front of screens. Even a moment outdoors can help you feel more grounded.

In a *Must Year*, you use nature as a simple, reliable support for your emotional and mental health, even if it's just stepping outside for a moment.

Today's Must Reflection

What is one small way you could connect with nature today, given where you live—and when will you do it?

DAY 145

Health & Vitality × Sleep Honesty

Sleep shapes nearly everything—your mood, energy, and clarity. Yet it is often the first thing sacrificed. You may insist you "don't need much sleep," while your body tells another story.

In a *Must Year*, you get honest about the rest you actually need and gently move your habits toward that truth.

Today's Must Reflection

Over the past week, how many hours of sleep did you *actually* get most nights—and how does that number feel in your body?

DAY 146

Career & Financial Well-Being × Identity as Learner

In a rapidly changing world, the most stable identity is often "I am a learner." Specific tools, roles, and industries shift, but the capacity to learn keeps you adaptable.

In a *Must Year*, you see yourself as someone who can grow skills at any age, rather than assuming, "I'm just not good at that."

Today's Must Reflection

In your current or desired field, what is one area where embracing "I am a learner here" would open more possibilities?

DAY 147

Love & Intimacy × Everyday Kindness

Grand gestures get attention, but everyday kindness—remembering details, offering help, softening your tone—does most of the work of sustaining love.

In a *Must Year*, you pay attention to small acts that say, "I see you," especially on ordinary days.

Today's Must Reflection

What is one specific, simple act of kindness you could offer to someone you love today?

DAY 148

Family, Friends & Community × Saying What You Mean

Hoping people will "just know" what you need often leads to frustration. Vague hints create confusion; clarity creates connection.

In a *Must Year*, you practice simple, direct statements—"I need…," "I feel…," "It would help me if…"—rather than expecting others to guess correctly.

Today's Must Reflection

Where have you been expecting someone to know what you need—and what is one clear sentence you could say instead?

DAY 149

Career Development & Meaningful Work × Impact on You

Purpose isn't only about how your work affects others; it also matters how your work shapes *you*. Does it align with your values? Does it grow you? Do you recognize yourself in the way you show up?

In a *Must Year*, you consider who you are becoming through your effort, not only what you produce.

Today's Must Reflection

How is your current work—or your current way of living—shaping you as a person, and do you like the direction?

DAY 150

Personal Growth & Learning × Milestone Check-In

Day 150 marks a genuine turning point. Even if your outer life hasn't dramatically changed, your inner life likely has. These shifts are the beginnings of a new normal.

In a *Must Year*, you pause to recognize change—however small—instead of focusing only on what remains undone. Recognition strengthens resolve.

Today's Must Reflection

Since beginning this journey, what are three specific changes—in how you think, feel, or act—that you're genuinely grateful for?

DAY 151

Spirituality & Inner Peace × Trust

Deep trust is the quiet belief that you can face what comes next—not because it will be easy, but because you will not be abandoned by your own strength, your faith, or those who support you. Without trust, every change feels like a threat.

In a *Must Year*, you clarify where you place your trust: routines, people, principles, faith, or something larger. Naming this can soften anxiety and guide difficult choices.

Today's Must Reflection

When life feels uncertain, what do you naturally lean on for steadiness—and does it truly support you?

DAY 152

Joy, Rest & Renewal × Micro Breaks

Rest doesn't always require a day off. "Micro breaks"—a quiet breath, a short stretch, standing up, stepping outside—can lower stress and reset your focus within minutes.

In a *Must Year*, you stop waiting for perfect conditions to rest. You learn to weave recovery into the margins of your day.

Today's Must Reflection

Where in today's schedule could you realistically insert two or three short micro-breaks—and what would you do in those moments?

DAY 153

Health & Vitality × Movement You Enjoy

Exercise often gets tied to guilt or pressure. But movement that you enjoy—walking, stretching, dancing, swimming, light strength work—is far more sustainable.

In a *Must Year*, you experiment until you find at least one form of movement that feels good enough that you don't dread it.

Today's Must Reflection

What is one type of movement you enjoy—or used to enjoy—and how could you include a small amount of it this week?

DAY 154

Career & Financial Well-Being × Story About Work

You carry a personal story about what work is for: survival, stability, achievement, service, expression, identity. That story affects how you feel every Monday morning.

In a *Must Year*, you question that story: Is my definition of work helping me become the person I want to be—or keeping me stuck?

Today's Must Reflection

Finish this sentence honestly: "Work, to me, is mostly about…" How does that belief shape your daily experience?

DAY 155

Love & Intimacy × Repair Attempts

After conflict, people often make "repair attempts"—small bids to reconnect: a touch, a message, a soft joke, a practical gesture. If these attempts are dismissed or ignored, distance grows.

In a *Must Year*, you learn to recognize both your repair attempts and those offered to you—and to respond in ways that reopen connection instead of reinforcing the break.

Today's Must Reflection

Think of a recent disagreement. Did you or the other person make any repair attempts—and how were they received?

DAY 156

Family, Friends & Community × Traditions

Traditions—recurring meals, calls, rituals, jokes, trips—create continuity and belonging. They don't have to be elaborate; even simple, repeated practices become meaningful over time.

In a *Must Year*, you consider which traditions you want to keep, release, or create anew to match the person you're becoming.

Today's Must Reflection

What is one simple tradition you'd like to create or revive with family or friends—and what is one small step toward starting it?

DAY 157

Career Development & Meaningful Work × Energy Test

Not every impressive opportunity is right for you. A simple test is noticing your energy: Do you feel more alive when you imagine doing this regularly, or heavier and drained?

In a *Must Year*, you let your honest energy response guide decisions instead of letting outside approval override your intuition.

Today's Must Reflection

Think of a path or project you're considering. When you imagine doing it week after week, does your body feel lighter, heavier, or neutral?

DAY 158

Personal Growth & Learning × Owning Wins

Some people minimize every improvement—"It's nothing," "I still have far to go"—without realizing they're starving their own motivation.

In a *Must Year*, you practice acknowledging your wins, however small, as evidence that change is alive and unfolding.

Today's Must Reflection

What is one win—tiny or significant—from the last week that you haven't allowed yourself to celebrate?

DAY 159

Spirituality & Inner Peace × Boundaries with Guilt

Guilt can be useful when it alerts you to something that needs repair. But "false guilt"—feeling bad simply for resting, having needs, or setting boundaries—is an unnecessary burden.

In a *Must Year*, you distinguish between helpful guilt ("I can fix this") and unhelpful guilt ("I'm bad for being human")—and refuse to let the second one lead your life.

Today's Must Reflection

Where do you most often feel guilty for things that are not actually wrong—and what truth could replace that guilt?

DAY 160

Joy, Rest & Renewal × Anticipation

Anticipation itself is a source of joy. Looking forward to something—a small outing, a treat, a conversation—brightens your mood long before it happens.

In a *Must Year*, you intentionally place small, life-giving events on your calendar so the future holds points of light instead of only obligations.

Today's Must Reflection

What is one simple, realistic thing you could plan for the next week that you would genuinely look forward to?

DAY 161

Health & Vitality × Check-In Questions

A simple internal check-in can keep you from running on empty. Questions like "How am I feeling physically?" or "What do I need right now?" bring awareness back into your body before exhaustion becomes a crisis.

In a *Must Year*, you build brief pauses into your day to ask these questions, instead of noticing your body only when it finally forces you to stop.

Today's Must Reflection

If you paused for 30 seconds right now and asked, "Body, what do you need?" what honest answer comes up first?

DAY 162

Career & Financial Well-Being × Short Term vs. Long Term

Some choices feel good now but cost you later; others feel uncomfortable now but serve your future. Without seeing both time horizons, it's easy to stay stuck in patterns that never move you forward.

In a *Must Year*, you ask both questions: "How will this feel today?" and "How will this look a year from now?" The combination brings wisdom to your decisions.

Today's Must Reflection

What is one money or career habit that feels easier now but will cost you later—and what is one small step toward reversing that pattern?

DAY 163

Love & Intimacy × Shared Responsibility

Relationships strain when one person silently carries most of the responsibility—planning, fixing, initiating, smoothing over. Even if the imbalance is unspoken, resentment begins to grow.

In a *Must Year*, you pay closer attention to how responsibilities are divided and open honest conversations about sharing the load more fairly.

Today's Must Reflection

In a close relationship, what is one area (planning, emotional support, chores, decisions) that feels unbalanced—and what honest conversation might help rebalance it?

DAY 164

Family, Friends & Community × Letting People Know You

People can only connect with the parts of you they can see. When you hide your real needs, struggles, questions, or hopes, others may assume you're fine when you're actually carrying more than you should alone.

In a *Must Year*, you practice letting trusted people see a little more of your inner world, instead of always performing the role they expect.

Today's Must Reflection

What is one true thing about your inner life right now that almost no one knows—and who might be safe enough to share even a small piece of it with?

DAY 165

Career Development & Meaningful Work × "Good Enough" Start

Waiting until you're fully confident or fully trained can delay your dreams indefinitely. Most meaningful work begins at the "good enough to start" stage—not the "perfectly prepared" stage.

In a *Must Year*, you permit yourself to begin small and imperfectly, trusting that you will gain clarity, courage, and skill along the way.

Today's Must Reflection

What is one project or change you could begin in a very small, "good enough" way this week instead of waiting to feel fully ready?

DAY 166

Personal Growth & Learning × Self-Observation

You learn a great deal about yourself simply by observing how you react—when you feel criticized, ignored, appreciated, tired, or overwhelmed. These reactions reveal your deeper needs and beliefs.

In a *Must Year*, you treat your behavior as data, not a verdict. You notice patterns without immediately shaming yourself for them.

Today's Must Reflection

In the last few days, what is one reaction you had that surprised you—and what might it reveal about what you needed or feared in that moment?

DAY 167

Spirituality & Inner Peace × Consistency Over Intensity

Powerful spiritual moments can be meaningful, but long-term inner peace usually comes from steady, consistent practices—brief reflection, prayer, meditation, or reading—done often rather than dramatically.

In a *Must Year*, you focus more on regular connection than on rare emotional intensity.

Today's Must Reflection

What is one brief, repeatable spiritual or reflective practice you could realistically do most days—and when would it fit best?

DAY 168

Joy, Rest & Renewal × Saying No to Fake Rest

Some activities look like rest but aren't—scrolling, background noise, habitual distractions, or "fun" that leaves you depleted. Fake rest fills time but doesn't restore you.

In a *Must Year*, you notice which activities truly refill you and gently reduce the ones that don't.

Today's Must Reflection

What is one thing you often do to "relax" that doesn't actually help—and what could you try instead that might restore you more deeply?

DAY 169

Health & Vitality × Compassion for Limits

You may get frustrated with your limits—strength, stamina, focus, stress tolerance. But treating your limits with contempt often leads to burnout, injury, or shame.

In a *Must Year*, you respect your limits as part of your humanity. You work with them and expand them slowly instead of pretending they don't exist.

Today's Must Reflection

Where have you been angry at your own limits lately—and what would it sound like to talk to yourself there with understanding instead?

DAY 170

Career & Financial Well-Being × Alignment with Values

There are many ways to make money; not all of them fit your values. When the way you earn and use money conflicts with what you believe, inner tension quietly grows.

In a *Must Year*, you regularly ask, "Does the way I earn and spend money reflect what I value?" Even tiny shifts toward alignment can bring relief and peace.

Today's Must Reflection

Name one value that matters to you (fairness, service, creativity, integrity). How well does your current work or money life express that value—and what is one tiny step toward closer alignment?

DAY 171

Love & Intimacy × Boundaries with Time

Being "always available" can feel loving at first, but over time it erodes your rest, focus, and sense of self. Healthy love honors the reality that each person has limited time and attention.

In a *Must Year*, you begin to protect certain blocks of time—sleep, work, rituals—so you can show up as your best self rather than a depleted one.

Today's Must Reflection

Where do you regularly give time you don't really have in a close relationship—and what is one small boundary that would still be loving but more realistic?

DAY 172

Family, Friends & Community × Roles You Want Now

You may have been the "strong one," "funny one," "responsible one," or "peacekeeper" for years. Those roles may no longer match who you want to be now.

In a *Must Year*, you ask not just, "Who have I been for them?" but also, "Who do I want to become now—for myself and for others?" This gently reshapes how you show up in long-standing relationships.

Today's Must Reflection

In your family or friend circle, what role would you *like* to grow into over the next few years—and what is one small action toward that shift?

DAY 173

Career Development & Meaningful Work × Obstacles as Information

Obstacles—lack of time, skill, support, or resources—can feel like signs to stop. Sometimes they are other times they are simply showing you what needs to change.

In a *Must Year*, you treat obstacles as information: "What is this revealing?" "What capacity needs strengthening?" "Is there another path?" You don't romanticize struggle, but you also don't assume it means "give up."

Today's Must Reflection

What is the biggest obstacle between you and a change you want to make—and what is it teaching you about what you need next?

DAY 174

Personal Growth & Learning × Repeating Lessons

When the same kinds of situations keep happening—similar conflicts, disappointments, or stuck points—it may be that life is presenting the same lesson until something changes within you.

In a *Must Year*, instead of asking only, "Why does this keep happening to me?" you also ask, "What have I not yet changed in myself or in my choices?"

Today's Must Reflection

What is one pattern you've seen repeat across different seasons or relationships—and what do you suspect this pattern is asking you to notice or change?

DAY 175

Spirituality & Inner Peace × Compassion for Others

Harsh judgments—seeing people as entirely lazy, selfish, or hopeless—often disturb your own peace as much as theirs. Compassion does not excuse behavior; it simply recognizes complexity.

In a *Must Year*, you experiment with seeing people as humans in process, not finished products. This softens your inner tension and can sometimes open new paths for connection.

Today's Must Reflection

Think of someone you find difficult to understand or forgive. What is one possible factor in their life that, if you knew it, would make their behavior more understandable—even if not acceptable?

DAY 176

Joy, Rest & Renewal × Variety

Doing the same "relaxing" activity every time—same show, same scrolling, same routine—eventually stops being restful. Your mind and body often need variety to truly reset.

In a *Must Year*, you create a simple menu of rest and play options, so you don't automatically default to the easiest but least satisfying choice.

Today's Must Reflection

List three different low-effort ways you could rest or have fun—and which one feels right for today?

DAY 177

Health & Vitality × Future Self

Your future body will live with the choices you make now—helpful or harmful. Imagining your future self can make today's decisions clearer and more grounded.

In a Must Year, you sometimes ask, "What would my future self-thank me for?" before choosing how to move, eat, sleep, or handle stress.

Today's Must Reflection

If you pictured yourself 5–10 years from now, what is one health or energy choice you could make today that version of you would be grateful for?

DAY 178

Career & Financial Well-Being × Asking for What You Want

You may hope others will notice your effort, offer opportunities, or give approval. Sometimes they do; often they don't.

In a *Must Year*, you practice respectfully asking—whether for information, mentorship, a chance to grow, or a different arrangement. You can't control the answer, but asking is part of owning your path.

Today's Must Reflection

What is one thing you wish someone would offer you in your work or financial life—and what would it look like to directly ask for it?

DAY 179

Love & Intimacy × Self-Soothing

Expecting a partner to calm every fear, regulate every mood, or fill every empty space is a burden no one can carry for long. Loving well also includes knowing how to soothe yourself.

In a *Must Year*, you develop simple self-soothing tools—breathing, grounding, journaling, a brief pause—so you bring more stability into love rather than relying on love to stabilize you.

Today's Must Reflection

When you feel upset in a close relationship, what is one healthy way you could calm yourself before or alongside talking with the other person?

DAY 180

Family, Friends & Community × Mid-Year Relational Review

By now, many days of reflection have touched your relationships. It's worth pausing to ask: What has actually changed in how you show up? What still needs care?

In a *Must Year*, this review is not about blame but about clarity—acknowledging progress and choosing your next small focus.

Today's Must Reflection

Looking at your relationships since beginning this journey, what is one way you've improved how you relate—and one area you want to grow in next?

Quarter 2 – Practicing New Ways of Being

You are now halfway through your *Must Year*.

In these middle months, the questions have shifted from "What is true?" to "What can I do differently, even a little?" You have explored:

- Saying no and yes more consciously.
- Testing new behaviors in health, money, and relationships.
- Speaking more directly about needs and limits.
- Naming new identity statements and casting small "votes" for them.

Quarter 2 is about **experiments and practice**. You have been invited to try new ways of being, not just think new thoughts.

Before you rush onward, pause with Days 91–180. Skim your entries. Look especially for:

- Moments you handled differently than your "old self" would have.
- Places where you set or considered boundaries.
- Signs of new courage, however small.

Season 2 Reflection

Consider writing about these:

1. Where did you attempt something new this quarter—an honest conversation, a boundary, a health choice, a money decision—that felt like a stretch?

2. Which of those experiments felt helpful or life-giving, even if imperfect?
3. Where did you feel tension between who you have been and who you are becoming?
4. When your "old script" was still pulling at you, what did it sound like—and how did you respond?
5. Looking ahead to the next 90 days, what is one behavior, practice, or boundary you want to keep strengthening?

The second quarter was not about getting everything right; it was about **showing up differently at least some of the time**. If you did that, even once, there is real change underway.

As you move into Quarter 3, the focus will turn more toward integration: seeing how shifts in one area ripple into others, and how your identity is consolidating across the whole of your life.

INTEGRATING A WHOLE LIFE

Alignment, Insight & Identity Consolidation (Days 181–270)

This is the season of coherence. The pieces of your life—identity, purpose, relationships, health, faith—begin to feel connected, not scattered. You notice how progress in one area supports the others, and you start living more from the center rather than the edges.

Quarter 3 is about harmony. You reclaim parts of yourself that were neglected and allow alignment to create more ease. This season brings a deeper sense of wholeness and groundedness. Your life begins to fit.

You're entering Quarter 3 — Integrating a Whole Life

DAY 181

Health & Vitality × Shame vs. Responsibility

Shame sounds like, "I'm disgusting," "I'm hopeless," or "I always fail." It attacks your identity and drains your energy. Responsibility sounds like, "This is where I am—here's one thing I can do next." It creates movement.

In a *Must Year*, you shift from shame about *who you are* to responsibility for *what you choose next*. That shift is where real change begins.

Today's Must Reflection

Where are you currently speaking to yourself with shame about your body or habits—and what would a more responsible, action-focused sentence sound like instead?

DAY 182

Career & Financial Well-Being × Multiple Roles

You may be an employee, parent, partner, caregiver, friend, creator—or several at once. Judging yourself as if you only carry one role creates unrealistic pressure and constant self-criticism.

In a *Must Year*, you consider your entire load when evaluating your progress, and you set expectations that match your real life—not a simplified version of it.

Today's Must Reflection

Considering all the roles you hold right now, are your expectations of yourself realistic—and what is one expectation you could gently loosen?

DAY 183

Love & Intimacy × Checking Assumptions

In relationships, you often react not to what was said, but to what you *assume* it meant—based on history, fears, or old wounds. These untested stories can create unnecessary conflict.

In a *Must Year*, you practice checking your interpretation: "When you said that, I took it to mean ____. Is that what you intended?" This simple step can dissolve tension instantly.

Today's Must Reflection

Think of a recent comment that hurt you. What did you assume it meant—and have you actually checked that assumption?

DAY 184

Family, Friends & Community × Support Style

People support in different ways: listening, problem solving, encouraging, giving practical help, or offering space. If you expect one style and receive another, you may feel uncared for even when the other person is genuinely trying.

In a *Must Year*, you notice how others naturally support and clarify the kind of support you personally need.

Today's Must Reflection

When you're struggling, what kind of support helps you most (listening, advice, practical help, space)—and have you clearly told your close people that?

DAY 185

Career Development & Meaningful Work × Seasonality

There are seasons when you can pour more energy into your calling, and seasons when circumstances limit how much you can do. Judging every season by your most productive one is unfair and unrealistic.

In a Must Year, you ask, "Given this season, what is a faithful way to show up for my purpose?" Sometimes that means bold growth; other times, gentle maintenance.

Today's Must Reflection

What season are you in right now—expanding, maintaining, or recovering—and what level of purpose-related action fits that season?

DAY 186

Personal Growth & Learning × Identity Around Emotions

If you label yourself as "too emotional," "overly sensitive," or "numb," those identities can become self-fulfilling. In reality, emotional skill is learnable—naming feelings, expressing them safely, and calming them.

In a Must Year, you stop treating your emotional patterns as fixed and begin seeing yourself as someone who can learn to relate to emotions differently.

Today's Must Reflection

How do you usually label yourself emotionally—and what more hopeful identity statement could you try instead?

DAY 187

Spirituality & Inner Peace × Making Amends

Sometimes inner unrest doesn't come from mystery—it comes from something unfinished: a hurt you caused and never addressed. Making amends, when safe and appropriate, can release long-held tension for both you and the other person.

In a *Must Year*, you consider where a sincere apology or act of repair could free your conscience and restore peace.

Today's Must Reflection

Is there one person you feel you wronged in a way that still weighs on you—and what would a thoughtful, respectful step toward amends look like?

DAY 188

Joy, Rest & Renewal × Boundaries with Productivity

If your worth is tied entirely to productivity, rest will always feel suspicious or "unearned." Over time, this mindset exhausts both your body and your joy.

In a *Must Year*, you begin separating your value from your output, allowing yourself real rest without guilt or self-attack.

Today's Must Reflection

When you try to rest, what productivity-based thought makes you feel guilty—and what truer statement about your worth could replace it?

DAY 189

Health & Vitality × Hydration & Basics

You may look for complex solutions while neglecting simple basics: water, regular meals, fresh air, gentle movement. These foundational inputs often have more impact than you expect.

In a *Must Year*, you return to the basics before assuming something is deeply wrong. You give your body what it clearly needs.

Today's Must Reflection

Which basic need—water, nourishment, movement, or fresh air—has been most ignored lately, and what is one small way you can meet it today?

DAY 190

Career & Financial Well-Being × Identity Around Worth

When your worth is tied to income, title, or status, any change in those areas can feel like a collapse of self. This makes risk, growth, and transition feel terrifying.

In a *Must Year*, you ground your worth in who you are and how you live—not only in what you earn or accomplish. This creates freedom to grow without fear.

Today's Must Reflection

How much do you secretly link your value as a person to your work or income—and what would it mean to start separating those in your own mind?

DAY 191

Health & Vitality × Identity Statements

How you describe yourself—"I'm lazy," "I'm disciplined," "I'm trying," "I'm done being careless"—quietly shapes how you treat your body. Identity statements function like internal instructions.

In a *Must Year*, you choose health-related identity statements that are honest yet hopeful, and you reinforce them with small actions that make those identities more true each day.

Today's Must Reflection

Finish this sentence: *"I am someone who, when it comes to my health, _____."* Does that sentence support you—or restrict you?

DAY 192

Career & Financial Well-Being × Risk Tolerance

Some people lean naturally toward risk; others value security above all. Ignoring your real risk tolerance can make you take leaps that feel terrifying—or stay in situations that quietly drain you.

In a *Must Year*, you get honest about how much risk you can hold right now and make decisions that stretch you slightly without overwhelming your nervous system.

Today's Must Reflection

On a scale from 1 (very risk-averse) to 10 (very risk-tolerant), where are you with work and money—and does your recent behavior reflect that number?

DAY 193

Love & Intimacy × Expressing Appreciation

You may feel grateful for your partner or loved one but rarely say it. Over time, unspoken appreciation can disappear beneath the noise of daily life.

In a *Must Year*, you practice expressing gratitude out loud so the people you care about don't have to guess how much they matter.

Today's Must Reflection

What is one recent thing your partner or a close person did that you genuinely appreciated—and how could you express that appreciation directly?

DAY 194

Family, Friends & Community × Emotional Safety Check

Some relationships feel safer for joy than for struggle—or the opposite. Emotional safety is not about perfection; it's about where you can show the full range of yourself.

In a *Must Year*, you notice where you feel safe, where you don't, and where you might gently test a bit more honesty.

Today's Must Reflection

Who in your life feels safest for sharing hard emotions—and is there someone you trust enough to reveal a little more of what's real?

DAY 195

Career Development & Meaningful Work × Alignment with Personality

Purpose looks different depending on your wiring—introverted or extroverted, detail-oriented or big-picture, fast-moving or slow-reflecting. Trying to live someone else's version of purpose feels like wearing the wrong size.

In a *Must Year*, you consider how your temperament fits your calling and look for expressions of purpose that feel natural to your personality.

Today's Must Reflection

How does your personality (e.g., introverted/extroverted, structured/flexible) fit—or clash—with the way you've been imagining your purpose?

DAY 196

Personal Growth & Learning × Values Clarification

Growth is easier when you know what you value. Without clarity, you may chase goals that impress others but leave *you* feeling empty or disconnected.

In a *Must Year*, you keep returning to questions like "What matters most to me?" and "What kind of person do I want to become?" These answers help guide your path.

Today's Must Reflection

Name three values you want your life to reflect more clearly (for example, courage, kindness, learning, freedom). How visible are they in your daily choices?

DAY 197

Spirituality & Inner Peace × "Who Am I Becoming?"

A powerful spiritual question is not "What am I getting from this?" but "Who am I becoming through this?" Circumstances shift, but the character you develop endures.

In a *Must Year*, you regularly step back and ask how your habits, reactions, and choices are shaping the deeper person you are becoming.

Today's Must Reflection

Looking at how you've handled stress, success, and relationships lately, who would you say you are becoming?

DAY 198

Joy, Rest & Renewal × Morning or Evening Joy

Many people save joy for weekends and miss the power of small daily rituals. A single moment of morning or evening enjoyment can shift the tone of your entire day.

In a *Must Year*, you create a simple "joy ritual" at the start or end of your day—tiny, consistent, and restorative.

Today's Must Reflection

What is one small, realistic morning or evening ritual that would add a moment of joy to your day?

DAY 199

Health & Vitality × Mental Narratives

The stories you tell about your health—"It's too late," "I always fail," "There's no point"—shape your behavior as much as any plan. A hopeless narrative sabotages progress before it begins.

In a *Must Year*, you catch these old narratives and begin rewriting them into statements that are truthful, compassionate, and more empowering.

Today's Must Reflection

What is one repeating sentence you tell yourself about your health or energy—and what revised sentence would be more accurate and helpful?

DAY 200

Career & Financial Well-Being × 200-Day Check-In

At 200 days, your external circumstances may or may not look dramatically different—but your awareness, identity, and clarity around work and money are likely. This is a natural moment to assess the shifts.

In a *Must Year*, you pause and honestly evaluate what has grown, what hasn't, and where you want to direct your energy next.

Today's Must Reflection

Since beginning this journey, what are two concrete ways your mindset or behavior around money or career have improved—and what is one area you want to focus on now?

DAY 201

Love & Intimacy × Boundaries Around the Past

Old wounds often echo into new relationships. But when you treat your current partner as if they *are* your past, both of you end up carrying weight that doesn't belong here.

In a *Must Year*, you notice when your reaction is more about an old story than today's person—and you gently name that difference instead of blending them together.

Today's Must Reflection

When you feel triggered in a current relationship, how much of the intensity is truly about this moment—and how much is leftover pain from before?

DAY 202

Family, Friends & Community × Saying "I Don't Know"

In families and friendships, you may feel pressure to provide certainty—answers, opinions, solutions. But "I don't know" can be disarming, honest, and deeply connective.

In a *Must Year*, you stop trying to be the expert on everyone's life. This creates more space for real listening and collaborative problem-solving.

Today's Must Reflection

Where in your relationships do you pretend to know more than you do—and what would it sound like to say, "I'm not sure, but I'm here with you"?

DAY 203

Career Development & Meaningful Work × Joy vs. Ego

Purpose can be fueled by joy—or by ego. Sometimes the desire to make an impact is partly the desire to be admired, validated, or impressive.

In a *Must Year*, you regularly check your motives: "Do I want this because it lights me up—or because I want to be seen a certain way?"

Today's Must Reflection

Think of a dream or goal you hold. How much of it is driven by genuine joy—and how much by wanting to prove something?

DAY 204

Personal Growth & Learning × Owning Your Preferences

Enjoying quiet more than crowds, structure more than spontaneity, or depth more than small talk are not flaws—they're preferences. Treating them as problems makes life feel off-key.

In a *Must Year*, you stop apologizing for your wiring and begin designing your days to include more of what fits you.

Today's Must Reflection

What is one personal preference you've been treating as a weakness—and how could you honor it in a small, practical way?

DAY 205

Spirituality & Inner Peace × Accepting Mixed Feelings

You can be grateful and still sad, hopeful and still scared, peaceful and still uncertain. Forcing yourself into one "acceptable" feeling creates inner conflict.

In a *Must Year*, you give yourself permission to hold mixed emotions, trusting that complexity is part of being fully human.

Today's Must Reflection

Where in your life do you feel two opposite emotions at once—and what changes when you allow both to exist instead of choosing one?

DAY 206

Joy, Rest & Renewal × Low-Cost Joy

Many people link joy with spending—trips, purchases, events. When money is tight, that belief can make life feel joyless.

In a *Must Year*, you rediscover low-cost or no-cost joys: a walk, music, conversation, creativity, reading, games, or small rituals that bring lightness back into ordinary days.

Today's Must Reflection

What is one enjoyable, low-cost activity you could do in the next few days?

DAY 207

Health & Vitality × All-or-Nothing Thinking

"All or nothing" thinking whispers, "If I can't do the full workout, it doesn't count," or "Since I slipped once, the whole day is ruined." This mindset quietly blocks progress.

In a *Must Year*, you practice "something is better than nothing." Ten minutes counts. One better choice counts. Resetting mid-day counts.

Today's Must Reflection

Where has all-or-nothing thinking been sabotaging your health—and what would a "something is better than nothing" option look like today?

DAY 208

Career & Financial Well-Being × Asking 'Is This Sustainable?'

You can push through intense seasons by willpower, but not every system is meant to be permanent. A schedule, workload, or money pattern that burns you out is not success—it's a warning.

In a *Must Year*, you ask, "Could I realistically live like this for another year?" The answer is valuable information.

Today's Must Reflection

What part of your current work or money routine clearly feels unsustainable—and what is one step toward something more livable?

DAY 209

Love & Intimacy × Celebrating Small Things

Waiting only for big milestones—anniversaries, trips, major achievements—can make every day love go unnoticed. Small moments also deserve celebration.

In a *Must Year*, you acknowledge small efforts, progress, and shared moments, not just the big events.

Today's Must Reflection

What is one small thing in a close relationship you could celebrate today instead of passing by?

DAY 210

Family, Friends & Community × Honest Capacity

You may say "yes" to plans or emotional support you don't truly have the capacity for. Over time, this leads to burnout, resentment, and inauthentic connection.

In a *Must Year*, you respond from honesty: "I care about you, and here's what I can realistically offer."

Today's Must Reflection

In the coming week, where do you need to be more honest about your emotional or time capacity—and what would that sound like spoken with kindness?

DAY 211

Health & Vitality × Identity Around Movement

You may see yourself as "not active," "not athletic," or "the sedentary one." These identity labels quietly discourage even small attempts at movement.

In a *Must Year*, you choose a new identity: "I am someone learning to move more." With that identity, every short walk, stretch, or moment you stand up becomes evidence, not an exception.

Today's Must Reflection

How do you usually describe yourself when it comes to movement—and what new, more supportive identity sentence could take its place?

DAY 212

Career & Financial Well-Being × Feeling Behind

Feeling "behind" often comes from comparing yourself to someone else's timeline, circumstances, or highlight reel. That pressure creates panic, not progress.

In a *Must Year*, you acknowledge where you are without shame and ask, "Given *my* real life and *my* values, what is the next wise step from here?"

Today's Must Reflection

Where do you most feel "behind" in work or money—and what is one small, concrete step forward based solely on your own pace?

DAY 213

Love & Intimacy × Respect

Lasting love is built on respect—seeing the other person as a full human being with their own needs, limits, and perspectives. Respect matters most when you're stressed or disappointed.

In a *Must Year*, you pay attention to whether your tone, words, and decisions reflect respect, especially in tense moments.

Today's Must Reflection

In a recent moment of tension, did your tone and words reflect respect—and what would you do differently if you could redo that moment?

DAY 214

Family, Friends & Community × Letting in Encouragement

You may absorb criticism easily but deflect encouragement—brushing off compliments, minimizing progress, or changing the subject. This makes it hard for good things to take root.

In a *Must Year*, you practice letting encouragement land. You don't need to fully believe it yet—you just stop pushing it away so quickly.

Today's Must Reflection

Recall something kind someone said about you recently. What would it feel like to sit with that statement for a full minute and consider that it might be true?

DAY 215

Career Development & Meaningful Work × Using What You Have

You may wait to start your calling until you have more time, money, credentials, or confidence. But many meaningful paths begin with what is already in your hands.

In a *Must Year*, you ask, "What can I do with what I have, from where I am?" and let that question guide small, real action.

Today's Must Reflection

List three resources you already have—skills, relationships, experiences, or tools. How could you use *one* of them this month toward something that matters to you?

DAY 216

Personal Growth & Learning × Owning Desires

It can feel safer to say you "don't really care" than to admit you deeply want something—connection, healing, stability, creativity, impact. Desire makes you vulnerable.

In a *Must Year*, you begin telling the truth to yourself about what you want. Honest desire gives direction to your growth.

Today's Must Reflection

What is one thing you deeply want but rarely admit—and what would it mean to simply acknowledge that desire as real?

DAY 217

Spirituality & Inner Peace × Humility

Humility is not thinking you are worthless; it is seeing yourself accurately—strengths, limitations, mistakes, and gifts—without pretending to be more or less.

In a *Must Year*, humility opens doors to learning, apologizing when needed, and receiving help—all of which support inner peace.

Today's Must Reflection

Where in your life would a little more humility help right now—asking for help, admitting a mistake, or accepting that you still have more to learn?

DAY 218

Joy, Rest & Renewal × Social Media

Social media can offer connection and entertainment, but it can also drain hours, increase comparison, and leave you more restless than before.

In a *Must Year*, you decide *how* and *when* you want to use it, instead of letting it fill every empty moment by default.

Today's Must Reflection

Over the last week, has social media mostly left you feeling better or worse—and what boundary could you test for the next few days?

DAY 219

Health & Vitality × Checking the "Why"

Every health habit—beneficial or harmful—serves a purpose: comfort, avoidance, reward, relief, control. Understanding the "why" gives you more power to change the "how."

In a *Must Year*, you gently ask, "What am I seeking through this habit—and is there a healthier way to meet that need?"

Today's Must Reflection

Choose one health habit you're unhappy with. What need is it trying to meet—and what healthier alternative could meet that same need?

DAY 220

Career & Financial Well-Being × Integrity with Promises

In work and financial matters, keeping your promises—to others and to yourself—builds trust and stability. Breaking them repeatedly erodes confidence and clarity.

In a *Must Year*, you promise less and follow through more, making your word something you can rely on.

Today's Must Reflection

What is one small promise—to yourself or someone else—you can realistically keep this week that would strengthen your sense of integrity?

DAY 221

Love & Intimacy × Honest Check-In with Self

You can work so hard on a relationship that you forget to ask a simpler question: "Do I *like* who I am here?" Effort matters, but not if it continually pulls you away from your core.

In a *Must Year*, you check in with yourself—not just the relationship: "Am I becoming more honest, more kind, more myself here…or less?"

Today's Must Reflection

In your closest relationship, do you like the version of yourself that most often shows up—and what, if anything, needs to shift?

DAY 222

Family, Friends & Community × Old Stories About You

Some people relate to you as if you are still who you were years ago—the angry one, the anxious one, the unreliable one, the quiet one. When you've outgrown those versions, their old story can feel suffocating.

In a *Must Year*, you gently speak and act in ways that reflect who you are now, even if others are slow to update their view.

Today's Must Reflection

What is one outdated story someone still seems to project onto you—and how could you gradually show them a truer version?

DAY 223

Career Development & Meaningful Work × Saying "This Is Not It"

Clarity sometimes comes not as a "yes," but as a firm "no." Admitting that a path is not right for you can feel like failure, but it is often valuable information.

In a *Must Year*, you release pursuits that clearly do not fit, freeing energy and space for what does.

Today's Must Reflection

Is there a path, role, or project you now know is not right for you—and what did it teach you about what *is* right?

DAY 224

Personal Growth & Learning × "Always" and "Never"

Words like "always" and "never" ("I always fail," "They never listen") are rarely true. They lock you into a rigid story that leaves little room for growth or nuance.

In a *Must Year*, you practice more precise language—"often," "sometimes," "in this situation"—which opens the possibility of change.

Today's Must Reflection

Where do you catch yourself using "always" or "never"—and what more accurate phrase could replace it?

DAY 225

Spirituality & Inner Peace × Gratitude for People

Gratitude is not only for things—it is also for people whose presence shaped, steadied, or inspired you, sometimes in quiet ways you barely noticed.

In a *Must Year*, you honor the humans who have been gifts along the way. Recognizing them softens your heart and strengthens connection.

Today's Must Reflection

Who is one person, past or present, whose presence has been a true gift—and what exactly did they give you?

DAY 226

Joy, Rest & Renewal × Play with Goals

Goals often feel serious and heavy. Adding a bit of play—experiments, visual tracking, small challenges—can reduce resistance and increase momentum.

In a *Must Year*, you allow creativity in how you pursue what matters so progress feels engaging rather than punishing.

Today's Must Reflection

What is one meaningful goal you have—and how could you make working toward it even slightly more playful or game-like?

DAY 227

Health & Vitality × Social Health

Your health is affected not just by food and movement but by the people around you. Supportive relationships can reduce stress and strengthen resilience; draining ones can do the opposite.

In a *Must Year*, you include "Who am I with?" in your definition of health.

Today's Must Reflection

Think of one relationship that calms you and one that tenses you. How might you gently increase exposure to the first and reduce the second?

DAY 228

Career & Financial Well-Being × "What Am I Learning Here?"

Even in seasons you don't want long term, there are lessons—about people, work, systems, boundaries, or yourself—that can serve you later.

In a *Must Year*, you ask, "While I am here, what can I learn that will help my future self?"

Today's Must Reflection

If your current work or financial season were a training ground, what do you suspect it is training you in?

DAY 229

Love & Intimacy × Boundaries with Technology

Phones, alerts, and constant access can quietly erode presence. Being physically near someone is not the same as being with them.

In a *Must Year*, you try simple tech boundaries—no phones during certain meals, device-free conversations, or protected time blocks—to reclaim true connection.

Today's Must Reflection

What is one specific tech boundary that would make your time with someone you love feel more connected?

DAY 230

Family, Friends & Community × Accepting Help

If you're used to being the helper, receiving help can feel uncomfortable—exposing, vulnerable, or like you're breaking your role.

In a *Must Year*, you remember that accepting help is an act of humility and trust—and it allows others to live their values too.

Today's Must Reflection

Where could you reasonably use help right now—and who might you reach out to, even if it feels a bit uncomfortable?

DAY 231

Health & Vitality × Recovery

Change is not only about how hard you push; it is equally about how well you recover. Muscles, minds, and emotions all need space to repair after effort.

In a *Must Year*, you begin seeing days of rest, lighter days, and gentler choices not as failure but as essential parts of a healthy training cycle for your whole life.

Today's Must Reflection

Where have you been pushing without true recovery—and what is one way you could build in more intentional recovery this week?

DAY 232

Career & Financial Well-Being × Clarity of "Why"

If you don't know *why* you want more money, a promotion, or a different role, you can chase them endlessly without ever feeling satisfied. Clear reasons guide better decisions.

In a *Must Year*, you keep asking, "What would this change actually give me—and is that truly what I want?"

Today's Must Reflection

Choose one financial or career goal you have. Why do you want it—what are you really hoping it will change in your life?

DAY 233

Love & Intimacy × Knowing Your Limits

Even in loving relationships, there are behaviors you cannot healthily accept—disrespect, manipulation, chronic dishonesty, or harm. Naming your limits is not unloving; it is protective.

In a *Must Year*, you grow clearer about what is negotiable and what is not in how you are treated.

Today's Must Reflection

What is one non-negotiable standard you have (or want to have) for how you are treated in intimate relationships?

DAY 234

Family, Friends & Community × Grief for What Isn't

Sometimes what hurts most in relationships is not what *is* there, but what never was—support you missed, words you needed, and the safety you didn't receive. Grieving that absence is part of healing.

In a *Must Year*, you allow yourself to name and feel that loss without getting stuck there, so you can choose how you want to relate now.

Today's Must Reflection

What is one thing you wish you had received from family or early friendships that you did not—and how has that shaped you?

DAY 235

Career Development & Meaningful Work × Quiet Impact

Not all purposes are loud or public. Some of the most meaningful contributions happen privately: raising children, caring for elderly people, mentoring quietly, or serving behind the scenes.

In a *Must Year*, you honor quiet impact as real impact—even if no one claps for it.

Today's Must Reflection

Where might you already be having a quiet, meaningful impact that you rarely recognize?

DAY 236

Personal Growth & Learning × Seeing Progress in Setbacks

Sometimes a "messy" reaction is progress. Speaking up awkwardly may be growth if you previously stayed silent. The form is imperfect, but the direction is new.

In a *Must Year*, you look for signs that even your missteps reflect a braver version of you than before.

Today's Must Reflection

Think of a recent situation you didn't handle perfectly. Is there any way your response still showed more growth than your past self would have?

DAY 237

Spirituality & Inner Peace × Letting Go of Control

Trying to make everything fit your plan creates constant tension—because life rarely obeys. Some peace comes from doing your part and releasing what you can't control.

In a *Must Year*, you practice acting where you have agency and loosening your grip where you don't.

Today's Must Reflection

Where are you currently trying to control something you genuinely cannot—and what would "doing my part and letting go of the rest" look like?

DAY 238

Joy, Rest & Renewal × Laughing

Laughter is a reset button for the nervous system. It eases tension, strengthens connection, and reminds you that life is more than your problems—even when they're real.

In a *Must Year*, you allow yourself to laugh, even in serious seasons, without feeling disloyal to your struggles.

Today's Must Reflection

When was the last time you laughed in a way that felt genuine—and what could you do today that *might* lead to that again?

DAY 239

Health & Vitality × Check for Overcomplication

Sometimes you get stuck planning elaborate routines instead of doing simple, helpful things—drinking water, walking, stretching, going to bed earlier. Overcomplication can be a form of avoidance.

In a *Must Year*, you ask, "What is the simplest helpful action I could take right now?" and start there.

Today's Must Reflection

In caring for your health, where might you be overcomplicating things—and what is one simple, obvious action you could take today?

DAY 240

Career & Financial Well-Being × Celebrating Milestones

Career and financial change can move slowly. If you only celebrate the final outcome, you may never feel enough momentum to continue.

In a *Must Year*, you mark milestones—debt reduced, a skill improved, a brave request made, a habit strengthened. These moments fuel the next stretch.

Today's Must Reflection

Looking back over the last few months, what is one career or money milestone—however small—you can pause to acknowledge and be proud of today?

DAY 241

Health & Vitality × Emotional Eating

Food often becomes a quick way to soften boredom, stress, or loneliness. The problem isn't seeking comfort—it's that the real need remains unaddressed while the habit deepens.

In a *Must Year*, you begin noticing when you eat for reasons other than hunger and gently ask, "What am I really needing right now?"

Today's Must Reflection

Think of a recent time you reached for food when you weren't truly hungry. What feeling were you trying to manage—and what else might have helped?

DAY 242

Career & Financial Well-Being × "Good Enough" Job vs. True Fit

A job can be "good enough" on paper—stable, decent pay—and still feel misaligned with who you are. Staying in that mismatch for too long can slowly numb you.

In a *Must Year*, you don't have to make sudden changes, but you do start telling the truth: "This works in some ways and not in others—and I'm allowed to explore options."

Today's Must Reflection

In your current work, what clearly *works* for you—and what clearly does *not*?

DAY 243

Love & Intimacy × Quality vs. Quantity of Time

You can spend hours with someone and still feel unseen, or share a short, focused moment and feel deeply connected. Connection is less about duration and more about presence.

In a *Must Year*, you aim for more moments of focused, genuine presence—even if they're brief—rather than long stretches of autopilot togetherness.

Today's Must Reflection

What is one way you could make even 15 minutes with someone you love feel more present and intentional?

DAY 244

Family, Friends & Community × Checking Your Story

When someone doesn't text back, cancels plans, or shows up differently than you hoped, your mind may rush to fill the gaps with a story: "They don't care," "They're mad," "I'm not important." Those are stories—not facts.

In a *Must Year*, you begin noticing when you're storytelling and consider other explanations before reacting.

Today's Must Reflection

Think of a recent disappointment with someone. What story did you tell yourself—and what else *might* be true?

DAY 245

Career Development & Meaningful Work × Ideal Day Exercise

Clarity often comes from imagining an ordinary ideal day—not a dream vacation, but the daily rhythms you'd love: how you work, who you see, how you rest.

In a *Must Year*, you sketch that day as a compass. It reveals your values, your desired pace, and the life you are quietly longing for.

Today's Must Reflection

If tomorrow were an ordinary but ideal day for you, how would it roughly look—from morning to night?

DAY 246

Personal Growth & Learning × Shadow Sides

Every strength has a shadow. Determination can turn into stubbornness; empathy into over-involvement; independence into isolation. Seeing this helps you use strengths wisely.

In a *Must Year*, you ask not only "What are my strengths?" but also "How do they go too far?"

Today's Must Reflection

Choose one strength you're proud of. In what ways can that same trait create difficulties when overused?

DAY 247

Spirituality & Inner Peace × Alignment with Daily Choices

Beliefs stay abstract until they shape behavior. Peace deepens when your choices reflect what you say matters—honesty, compassion, faith, integrity—especially in small moments.

In a *Must Year*, you let your deepest convictions quietly guide your calendar, tone, and responses—not just your opinions.

Today's Must Reflection

Choose one principle you say matters to you. How clearly has it shown up in your behavior this past week?

DAY 248

Joy, Rest & Renewal × Protecting One Thing

Trying to overhaul your rest and joy all at once often leads to abandoning the plan. Protecting even *one* small, regular source of enjoyment can change your emotional landscape.

In a *Must Year*, you choose one practice—coffee with a friend, a hobby block, a quiet hour—and treat it as necessary, not optional.

Today's Must Reflection

What is one enjoyable practice you're willing to protect on your calendar for the next month?

DAY 249

Health & Vitality × Identity Around "Slips"

When you miss a workout, overeat, or stay up too late, you can interpret it as proof you can't change—or as a single slip in a much longer story of growth.

In a *Must Year*, you see slips as moments, not identities. You simply return to the path without the extra narrative.

Today's Must Reflection

Think of a recent "slip" with your health. What story did you tell about yourself—and what more helpful story could you choose instead?

DAY 250

Career & Financial Well-Being × Interconnected Wheel

Career, finances, health, relationships, personal growth, fun, and spirituality all affect each other like spokes in a wheel. A shift in one area often ripples through the others.

In a *Must Year*, you ask, "If I change this one thing, how will it affect the rest of my life?" Seeing the whole picture leads to wiser decisions.

Today's Must Reflection

Pick one area you're considering changing. How might that change positively (or negatively) affect two other areas of your life?

DAY 251

Love & Intimacy × Speaking Up Earlier

Small annoyances or hurts, when unspoken, often grow into large explosions. The real issue is rarely the original moment—it's how long it sat unheard.

In a *Must Year*, you practice speaking up sooner, in calmer tones, about small things so they don't have to become big things.

Today's Must Reflection

What is one small frustration or need you've been holding in—and how could you express it simply and respectfully?

DAY 252

Family, Friends & Community × Mixed Roles

A friend may feel like family, and a family member may function more like a distant acquaintance. Expecting people to fill roles they can't—or won't—fill creates quiet, lingering pain.

In a *Must Year*, you allow relationships to be what they truly are, not only what you wish they were, and you adjust your expectations accordingly.

Today's Must Reflection

Is there someone you expect to act like "family" who consistently behaves more like a looser connection—and what boundary or mindset shift might help?

DAY 253

Career Development & Meaningful Work × "Who Do I Help?"

A practical way to clarify your calling is to ask: "Who do I naturally help?" Children, clients, coworkers, beginners, people in crisis—your pattern is data.

In a *Must Year*, you pay attention to who benefits most from your presence and skills. Purpose often lives near the people you instinctively serve.

Today's Must Reflection

Looking back over your life, what kind of person have you most often helped or been drawn to support?

DAY 254

Personal Growth & Learning × Journaling as Mirror

Writing down your thoughts can reveal patterns you can't see when everything stays inside your mind. It turns vague discomfort into something visible and workable.

In a *Must Year*, even a few lines of honest writing can act as a mirror, clarifying what's really happening within you.

Today's Must Reflection

If you wrote freely for five minutes about whatever is on your mind today, what topic or feeling do you suspect would appear most?

DAY 255

Spirituality & Inner Peace × Daily "Reset"

Days rarely unfold perfectly. A rough morning or conflict can make you want to abandon the whole day. But you can choose a reset—midday, afternoon, or evening—where you start again on purpose.

In a *Must Year*, each reset becomes a small act of faith: that the rest of the day is still worth showing up for.

Today's Must Reflection

When things go off track, what would a simple reset ritual look like for you—a breath, a phrase, a brief pause?

DAY 256

Joy, Rest & Renewal × Shared Joy

Some experiences are simply better shared—a meal, a joke, a walk, a movie, a game. Shared joy strengthens bonds and reminds you that you're not carrying life alone.

In a *Must Year*, you protect space not only for solo rest but also for simple shared enjoyment with safe people.

Today's Must Reflection

Who is one person you genuinely enjoy spending time with—and what's one small, fun thing you could invite them to do with you?

DAY 257

Health & Vitality × Energy Audit

Different activities affect your energy differently. Some leave you clearer; others leave you drained. Without noticing this, you can unintentionally fill your days with what exhausts you.

In a *Must Year*, you ask, "What gives me energy? What takes it away?" and adjust where you can.

Today's Must Reflection

List three things from the last week that clearly boosted your energy and three that clearly drained it. What pattern do you notice?

DAY 258

Career & Financial Well-Being × Asking for Feedback

Feedback can feel intimidating, but it often reveals how others see your strengths and where you can grow. Without it, you may operate on outdated assumptions.

In a *Must Year*, you selectively ask trusted people, "What am I doing well?" and "Where could I improve?" treating their insight as information, not judgment.

Today's Must Reflection

Who is one person you trust to give you honest, constructive feedback—and what is one specific question you could ask them?

DAY 259

Love & Intimacy × Owning Your Choices

It's easy to say, "You made me feel…" or "You made me do…" yet your reactions are still your choices. Owning that gives you power to change them.

In a *Must Year*, you shift from "You always…" to "When this happens, I feel… and I choose…" which creates healthier conversations.

Today's Must Reflection

Think of a recent conflict. What did *you* choose to say or do that you can own—and how might you choose differently next time?

DAY 260

Family, Friends & Community × Legacy Through Presence

Years from now, people will remember far less about your opinions and far more about how it *felt* to be around you—especially during hard seasons.

In a *Must Year*, you ask, "What kind of memory am I creating in these relationships right now?" and let that awareness guide your small, daily behaviors.

Today's Must Reflection

If someone described how you typically treat them, what would you *hope* they say—and what is one small action today that supports that?

DAY 261

Health & Vitality × Saying "I'm Not Fine"

Automatically responding "I'm fine" when you're exhausted, overwhelmed, or in pain disconnects you from support and from your own truth. It also trains people not to look deeper.

In a *Must Year*, you practice occasionally saying, "I'm a bit worn down today," or "I'm struggling with…"—to at least one safe person, and to yourself.

Today's Must Reflection

Where do you most often pretend to be "fine" when you're not—and what would a slightly truer answer sound like?

DAY 262

Career & Financial Well-Being × Side Projects

Your main job may not carry all of your interests or sense of purpose. A small side project—paid or unpaid—can offer room to explore, create, or serve in new ways.

In a *Must Year*, you consider whether adding a modest side project might increase your overall satisfaction.

Today's Must Reflection

Is there a small creative, service-oriented, or entrepreneurial project outside your main work that you feel drawn to experiment with?

DAY 263

Love & Intimacy × Showing Your Effort

You may make quiet efforts your partner never sees—internal shifts, resisted impulses, changed habits. If they don't know, they can't appreciate them.

In a *Must Year*, you sometimes name your effort: "I'm really trying to…" Not as a bid for praise, but as a way of letting each other in.

Today's Must Reflection

What is one change you've been genuinely trying to make in how you love—and have you clearly shared that effort with the other person?

DAY 264

Family, Friends & Community × Emotional Boundaries

You can care deeply about someone without absorbing every mood they have. Taking full responsibility for others' emotions often leads to burnout and resentment.

In a *Must Year*, you practice distinguishing between empathy ("I feel with you") and enmeshment ("I feel your emotions instead of my own").

Today's Must Reflection

With whom do you most often take on emotions that aren't yours—and what might a healthier emotional boundary look like?

DAY 265

Career Development & Meaningful Work × Doubt as Companion

Doubt almost always walks beside real purpose. If you wait for doubt to disappear before you move, you may never begin at all.

In a *Must Year*, you treat doubt as a normal companion—not a stop sign. You move with it, not after it's gone.

Today's Must Reflection

Where are you waiting for complete confidence before taking a step—and what is one action you could take *with* doubt still present?

DAY 266

Personal Growth & Learning × Honoring Limits While Growing

You can stretch yourself without tearing yourself. Pushing far beyond your emotional or physical limits too quickly can cause you to snap back harder.

In a *Must Year*, you look for your growth edge—the place where challenge is real but not crushing—and work there consistently.

Today's Must Reflection

In one area of growth, what feels like a realistic "edge" right now—not too easy, not overwhelming?

DAY 267

Spirituality & Inner Peace × Practicing Presence

Much anxiety comes from mentally living in the future or the past. Even a few moments of presence—feeling your breath, observing your surroundings, focusing on a single task—can interrupt the spiral.

In a *Must Year*, you build small pockets of presence into your day as both a spiritual and practical exercise.

Today's Must Reflection

What is one activity today—eating, walking, talking, working—that you could choose to do with full attention for a few minutes?

DAY 268

Joy, Rest & Renewal × Letting Yourself Enjoy

When life has been hard for a long time, feeling good can even feel unsafe. You might cut off joy quickly, waiting for the next problem.

In a *Must Year*, you allow yourself to think, "This moment is actually okay," and stay in that feeling a bit longer.

Today's Must Reflection

When something feels genuinely good, do you let yourself enjoy it—or do you rush past it? What would it look like to linger 30 seconds longer?

DAY 269

Health & Vitality × Asking for Practical Help

Health changes are easier with support—someone to walk with, swap meal ideas, offer reminders, or hold you kindly accountable. Doing everything alone adds unnecessary strain.

In a *Must Year*, you consider inviting a trusted person into your health goals in a concrete way.

Today's Must Reflection

Who is one person you could ask for a small, specific kind of support with your health—and what exactly would you ask for?

DAY 270

Career & Financial Well-Being × Mid-Course Correction

You don't have to keep a plan simply because it was yours. As you learn more, you're allowed to adjust course without seeing it as failure.

In a *Must Year*, you revisit your earlier work and money intentions and ask, "Given what I know now, what needs updating?"

Today's Must Reflection

Looking back at how you imagined your work or finances at the start of the year, what is one part of your plan that now needs adjustment?

Quarter 3 – Integrating a Whole Life

You are three quarters of the way through your *Must Year*.

In this season, the questions have stepped back more often to look at the big picture:

- How your choices in one area affect the others.
- How your identity statements are showing up across domains.
- How your circle of people, your work, your habits, and your beliefs are starting to align—or clash.

Quarter 3 is about **integration**. Instead of treating health, money, love, work, and spirituality as separate projects, you have begun to see them as parts of a single story: your life.

Take some time with Days 181–270. As you skim:

- Notice where themes from earlier quarters (boundaries, shame, desire, rest, purpose) are now weaving together.
- Notice which relationships, habits, or beliefs have shifted position in your life—closer to the center or further from it.

Season 3 Reflection

Write about any of the following:

1. Where do you see the clearest signs that your life is becoming more aligned—your time, energy, and values pointing in the same direction?
2. Where are you still living a "split life," saying one thing matters and living as if something else does?

3. Which relationships feel more honest now than they did at the start of the year? Which feel more strained—and what might that be telling you?
4. What identity sentence about yourself ("I am someone who…") feels truer now than it did a few months ago?
5. As you approach the final quarter, what do you most want to **understand**, not just change?

In the next 90 days, the questions will guide you into deliberate closure and forward intention: noticing what this year has actually done in you and deciding what you want to carry into the next chapter.

You are not at the finish line. You are at a vantage point. Look at how far you have come.

CLOSING AND BEGINNING

This is the season of reflection, gratitude, and renewal.

You will look back with honesty and compassion – acknowledging what grew, what softened, what healed, and what still calls to you.

Season 4 is a sacred threshold. You complete the year not by looking for what is missing but by looking for what has been found.

This season honors both endings and beginnings. You finish with clarity and step forward with intention.

Review, Release & Forward Intention (Days 271–360)

This is the season of closure and new beginnings. Over these final months, you gather what the year has taught you—about your identity, your relationships, your work, your health, your faith, your rest—and decide what comes with you and what you are ready to release.

Quarter 4 is about honest review and intentional transition. You name the gains and the griefs, turn regrets into lessons, and clarify how you want to live the next chapter. As you move toward Year's End, your questions become: "What am I grateful for? What am I done carrying? Who am I becoming next?"

You're entering Quarter 4 — Closing and Beginning

DAY 271

Love & Intimacy × Honest Desires

You may hint, withdraw, or criticize when what you really feel is, "I wish we were closer," "I miss you," or "I need more from us." Indirect signals rarely create the connection you want.

In a *Must Year*, you practice naming your desires plainly, without demand: "I'd love more time together," or "I miss talking deeply with you."

Today's Must Reflection

What is one honest desire you have in a close relationship that you haven't expressed clearly yet?

DAY 272

Family, Friends & Community × Fair Expectations

Expecting one person to meet all of your emotional, social, and practical needs is heavy for them and limiting for you. Different relationships can meet different needs.

In a *Must Year*, you spread your needs more realistically—some friends for depth, some for fun, some for shared history—rather than overloading one person.

Today's Must Reflection

Where might you be expecting too much from one relationship—and what other sources of support or connection could you cultivate?

DAY 273

Career Development & Meaningful Work × Being a Beginner Again

Starting something new later in life can feel uncomfortable—you're used to competence, and now you feel clumsy. Yet willingness to be a beginner is often the doorway to fresh purpose.

In a *Must Year*, you allow yourself to learn out loud, make mistakes, and be new at things without labeling yourself as "behind."

Today's Must Reflection

What is one area you feel drawn to learn in—even if it means being a visible beginner?

DAY 274

Personal Growth & Learning × Tiny Experiments

You don't need a massive commitment to learn something new about yourself. Small experiments—trying a new routine for a week, responding differently in a conflict, or organizing your day in a new way—can reveal a lot.

In a *Must Year*, you replace some overthinking with gentle trials: "Let me test this and see what happens."

Today's Must Reflection

What is one tiny experiment you could try this week in how you think, respond, or structure your time?

DAY 275

Spirituality & Inner Peace × Practicing Acceptance

Acceptance is not approval. It is simply acknowledging that something is what it is *right now*, which is the only starting point from which change or peace becomes possible.

In a *Must Year*, you practice saying, "This is what's real in this moment," before deciding what comes next.

Today's Must Reflection

What is one situation you've been resisting or denying—and what would it sound like to state the truth about it without judgment?

DAY 276

Joy, Rest & Renewal × Body-Based Rest

Not all rest is mental. Your body also needs low-demand time—stretching, baths, slow walks, or simple stillness—where it is not bracing or rushing.

In a *Must Year*, you explore what physical rest looks like for you, not just mental distraction.

Today's Must Reflection

What is one body-focused form of rest you could try today—stretching, a slow walk, or a warm shower taken without rushing?

DAY 277

Health & Vitality × Preventive Care

It's tempting to see doctors, therapists, or checkups only when something is obviously wrong. Preventive care can feel unnecessary—until you wish you had done it earlier.

In a *Must Year*, you view routine checkups and early conversations as acts of respect for your future self.

Today's Must Reflection

Is there a preventive appointment (medical, dental, mental health) you've been postponing—and what is your next concrete step to schedule it?

DAY 278

Career & Financial Well-Being × Multiple Streams

Relying on a single income source can feel vulnerable, especially in changing industries. Even a very small second stream—freelancing, teaching, selling something simple—can increase resilience.

In a *Must Year*, you consider whether an additional, manageable income stream fits your life and values.

Today's Must Reflection

What is one skill, product, or service you could *imagine* earning a little extra from—even if you're not ready to act yet?

DAY 279

Love & Intimacy × Knowing When to Pause

In heated moments, staying in the conversation can do more harm than good. A wise pause protects the relationship when you're too triggered to speak well.

In a *Must Year*, you learn to say, "I care about this, and I need a short break, so I don't say something I regret."

Today's Must Reflection

In your last conflict, would a brief pause have helped—and how could you request one in a healthy way next time?

DAY 280

Family, Friends & Community × 280-Day Relational Review

At 280 days, you've practiced many small shifts in how you relate. Some relationships may feel lighter; others may reveal deeper issues. Both are valuable information.

In a *Must Year*, you pause to notice which connections are growing with you, which are straining, and what that suggests for your next steps.

Today's Must Reflection

Which relationship has improved most for you this year so far—and which one now needs the most honest attention or boundary?

DAY 281

Health & Vitality × Movement Breaks

Long stretches of sitting—even with good intentions—leave your body stiff and your mind foggy. Short movement breaks—standing, stretching, walking—can reset both.

In a *Must Year*, you treat small movement moments as real care, not interruptions of "real" work.

Today's Must Reflection

Where in your day could you realistically add two or three short movement breaks—and what would each one look like?

DAY 282

Career & Financial Well-Being × Values Check

You can excel at something that doesn't match your values. Over time, doing good work that conflicts with what you believe can quietly drain you.

In a *Must Year*, you regularly ask, "Does what I *do*, and how I do it, reflect what I actually stand for?"

Today's Must Reflection

Choose one value that matters to you. How well does your current work or money life support—or undermine—that value?

DAY 283

Love & Intimacy × Listening to Your Body

Your body often reacts in relationships before your mind finds words: a knot in your stomach, tight chest, shallow breathing, or a sense of ease and warmth. These signals are data.

In a *Must Year*, you include your body's cues as part of how you read the health of your intimate connections.

Today's Must Reflection

When you're with someone close to you, what does your body typically do—relax, tense, speed up, go numb—and what might that be telling you?

DAY 284

Family, Friends & Community × Small Reaches

Not every act of connection has to be deep or long. A brief text, photo, check-in, or "thinking of you" keeps bonds alive between bigger conversations.

In a *Must Year*, you use small, genuine reaches to maintain and warm your circle.

Today's Must Reflection

Who is one person you care about but haven't contacted in a while—and what is one very small reach you could make today?

DAY 285

Career Development & Meaningful Work × Season of Preparation

Some seasons are less about visible output and more about preparation—learning, healing, saving, building skills or relationships. They feel slow but are often essential.

In a *Must Year*, you honor preparation as real work toward your calling, not "wasted time."

Today's Must Reflection

If this is a preparation season for you, what are you preparing—skills, stability, clarity, courage?

DAY 286

Personal Growth & Learning × Self-Respect

Self-respect grows when your actions match what you know is right for you. Every time you keep a boundary, tell the truth, or follow through, you whisper to yourself, "I can count on me."

In a *Must Year*, you treat small acts of integrity as deposits into your self-respect.

Today's Must Reflection

What is one recent choice you made that increased your respect for yourself—and what similar choice could you make again this week?

DAY 287

Spirituality & Inner Peace × Simple Gratitude Practice

Big spiritual practices can feel overwhelming. A simple daily habit—naming three things you're grateful for, or one way you were helped—can gently shift your focus over time.

In a *Must Year*, you let simple, repeatable gratitude quiet your mind.

Today's Must Reflection

Right now, what are three specific things from the last 24 hours—however small—you can honestly feel grateful for?

DAY 288

Joy, Rest & Renewal × Saying Yes to Invitations

Automatically declining invitations because you're tired, anxious, or out of practice can slowly shrink your life. Occasionally saying yes can reopen your world.

In a *Must Year*, you don't say yes to everything, but you do consider whether some invitations are opportunities to feel more alive.

Today's Must Reflection

Is there an upcoming invitation you're tempted to decline by habit—but that might genuinely do you good if you said yes?

DAY 289

Health & Vitality × Gentle Mornings

The first moments of your day set a tone—rushed and harsh, or slightly more grounded. Even small changes—less phone, lighter, or quiet—can help.

In a *Must Year*, you experiment with making your mornings 5–10% kinder to your body and mind.

Today's Must Reflection

What is one small change you could make tomorrow morning that would make the start of your day feel slightly less stressful?

DAY 290

Career & Financial Well-Being × 290-Day Reality Check

By now, you've seen more of your patterns with work and money—strengths, fears, improvements, and stuck points. Avoiding reality won't help, facing it will.

In a *Must Year*, you ask, "Given what I now know about myself here, what honest adjustment do I need to make?"

Today's Must Reflection

What is one clear truth you now see about your relationship with work or money—and what is one small, concrete action that responds to that truth?

DAY 291

Love & Intimacy × Shared Responsibility for Growth

Sometimes one person in a relationship becomes the "growth engine"—reading, reflecting, initiating change—while the other stays mostly the same. Over time, this imbalance can feel lonely and discouraging.

In a *Must Year*, you remember that healthy relationships require two people taking some responsibility for their own growth. One person cannot drag the entire process alone.

Today's Must Reflection

In your closest relationship, are both of you taking responsibility for growth—or does it feel one-sided, and how?

DAY 292

Family, Friends & Community × Checking for Resentment

Resentment often signals that a boundary is needed or has been crossed. Ignoring it doesn't make it disappear; it simply leaks out through distance, sarcasm, or burnout.

In a *Must Year*, you treat resentment as useful information—a call to pause, reflect, and possibly reset how you're relating.

Today's Must Reflection

Where do you feel a quiet resentment toward someone you care about—and what boundary or honest conversation might that feeling be asking for?

DAY 293

Career Development & Meaningful Work × Using Your Story

Your past struggles, detours, and recoveries can become tools for serving others. What you've lived through often equips you to help in ways theory cannot.

In a *Must Year*, you consider that your story isn't only something you survived—it may also be something you can *use* for good.

Today's Must Reflection

What is one hard thing you've come through that might someday help you support someone facing something similar?

DAY 294

Personal Growth & Learning × Accepting "Good Enough" Days

Not every day will be a peak day. Some days will simply be "good enough"—a few solid choices, a bit of effort, some rest. That is still real progress.

In a *Must Year*, you allow yourself average days without declaring the whole journey a failure.

Today's Must Reflection

What would a "good enough" day look like for you today—and can you allow that to count?

DAY 295

Spirituality & Inner Peace × Making Space for Awe

Awe can come from many places—nature, music, art, courage, kindness, meaningful connection. These moments remind you that life is larger than your routines and worries.

In a *Must Year*, you occasionally seek out or at least notice moments that move you beyond the everyday.

Today's Must Reflection

When was the last time you felt genuine awe—and what is one simple way you could invite that feeling again?

DAY 296

Joy, Rest & Renewal × Protecting Sleep from Entertainment

Late-night entertainment—shows, scrolling, games—can feel like "me time," but usually steals sleep and leaves you more drained the next day.

In a *Must Year*, you weigh the short-term pleasure of one more episode against the long-term benefit of better rest.

Today's Must Reflection

How often do you trade sleep for late-night entertainment—and what is one limit you'd be willing to test this week?

DAY 297

Health & Vitality × Celebrating Non-Scale Wins

Health progress appears in many forms: stamina, clearer thinking, improved labs, calmer mood, steadier habits, stronger boundaries. Weight and appearance are only one small part.

In a *Must Year*, you celebrate these non-scale wins as real evidence of change.

Today's Must Reflection

What is one improvement in your health or energy that has nothing to do with a number on a scale?

DAY 298

Career & Financial Well-Being × Asking "What If I'm Wrong?"

Some of your strongest beliefs about work and money—"I have to do everything alone," "I'm terrible with money," "this is the only path"—are untested assumptions.

In a *Must Year*, you occasionally ask, "What if I'm at least partly wrong about this?" to open new possibilities.

Today's Must Reflection

What is one strong belief you hold about your work or finances—and what might change if it turned out not to be fully true?

DAY 299

Love & Intimacy × Noticing What's Working

Focusing only on what's missing in your relationship can make you blind to what *is* working: small kindnesses, effort, steadiness, shared humor. Seeing both gives a fuller, fairer picture.

In a *Must Year*, you intentionally notice—and sometimes name—what is going well, not just what needs repair.

Today's Must Reflection

List three specific things that *are* working in a close relationship right now, even if other parts feel difficult.

DAY 300

Family, Friends & Community × 300-Day Gratitude

At 300 days, many people have shaped your path—supporting, challenging, teaching, encouraging, or simply being present. Recognizing this web of connection strengthens your sense of belonging.

In a *Must Year*, you pause to thank, at least in your heart—and maybe directly—the people whose presence has helped you become more of who you are meant to be.

Today's Must Reflection

Who are three people you feel genuinely grateful for in this season—and what have they each added to your life?

DAY 301

Health & Vitality × Listening to Fatigue Early

Fatigue is often one of your body's most honest signals. Before burnout shows up as illness or emotional collapse, it usually appears as subtle exhaustion, irritability, or mental fog.

In a Must Year, you stop waiting for "absolute depletion" before adjusting. You learn to listen when your body whispers—not only when it finally screams.

Today's Must Reflection

Over the last week, what was one moment your body hinted that you were tired earlier than you admitted—and what small adjustment could you have made right then?

DAY 302

Career & Financial Well-Being × Healthy Ambition

Ambition can expand your life or exhaust it. When ambition flows from purpose, it energizes you. When it flows from insecurity, comparison, or fear, it drains you.

In a *Must Year*, you ask not "How much more can I cram in?" but "Does this ambition honor who I'm becoming?"

Today's Must Reflection

Think of one ambition you hold. What part of that desire feels grounded and healthy—and what part might be driven by pressure or comparison?

DAY 303

Love & Intimacy × Receiving Love

Many people know how to love but struggle to *receive* love—compliments, care, affection, or support. When you deflect it, you unintentionally block connection.

In a *Must Year*, you practice letting yourself be loved without pushing it away, minimizing it, or assuming it's undeserved.

Today's Must Reflection

When someone tries to love you—through words, gestures, or attention—how do you usually respond? What would "receiving" look like?

DAY 304

Family, Friends & Community × Repair After Distance

Life seasons, disagreements, or neglect can create distance between you and someone you care about. Repair doesn't require perfection—just presence, sincerity, and a small reach.

In a *Must Year*, you don't wait for the perfect moment or speech. You take one step toward rebuilding connection where it still matters.

Today's Must Reflection

Who is one person you feel distance from but still value—and what gentle first reach could you make without expectation?

DAY 305

Career Development & Meaningful Work × Courage to Pivot

Sometimes the bravest part of purpose is choosing to pivot—changing directions even when you've invested years into a path that no longer fits.

In a *Must Year*, you honor both your past effort and your evolving truth. You allow yourself to shift toward what aligns now.

Today's Must Reflection

Is there one area of your work where a pivot (small or large) is beginning to feel necessary—and what is the smallest experiment toward that new direction?

DAY 306

Personal Growth & Learning × Letting Go of Old Identities

Old identities—"the fixer," "the strong one," "the quiet one," "the successful one"—may have helped you survive past seasons but can limit who you are becoming.

In a *Must Year*, you respectfully retire identities that no longer serve you and allow new ones to take shape.

Today's Must Reflection

What is one outdated identity you still carry—and what might its healthier, updated version be?

DAY 307

Spirituality & Inner Peace × Returning to Center

No matter how grounded your practices are, life will pull you off center—stress, conflict, deadlines, emotion. Peace isn't about never losing center; it's about knowing how to return.

In a *Must Year*, you identify what brings you back—prayer, breath, scripture, silence, music, nature—and you use it intentionally.

Today's Must Reflection

When you feel scattered or overwhelmed, what reliably brings you back to center—and when was the last time you intentionally used it?

DAY 308

Joy, Rest & Renewal × Permission to Do Nothing

Doing nothing is different from being lazy. "Nothing time" is unscheduled, quiet space that allows creativity, restoration, and emotional reset.

In a Must Year, you stop equating rest with failure. You treat intentional "nothing" as part of a well-lived life.

Today's Must Reflection

If you gave yourself one guilt-free hour of "doing nothing," what would that actually look like for you?

DAY 309

Health & Vitality × Reducing Hidden Stressors

Not all stress is loud. Some of it hides in clutter, unresolved tasks, ongoing conflict, disorganization, or too many micro-decisions. These small stressors accumulate silently.

In a *Must Year*, you identify the tiny stressors you can actually fix—and reduce them one by one.

Today's Must Reflection

What is one small but persistent stressor (a task, mess, decision, or tension) that drains you more than you admit—and what is one simple step toward reducing it?

DAY 310

Career & Financial Well-Being × Letting Yourself Dream Again

Practicality is necessary, but if you silence your long-term dreams for too long, your work life can shrink into mere survival.

In a Must Year, you revisit the dreams you shelved—not to chase all of them at once, but to remember what lights you up and to see whether any piece of them deserves new life.

Today's Must Reflection

What is one career or financial dream you once held that still sparks something in you—and what tiny step could reconnect you to that dream?

DAY 311

Health & Vitality × Year to Date View

Day to day, it can be hard to see health progress. A wider window—months instead of hours—often reveals subtle but meaningful shifts in energy, awareness, boundaries, and habits.

In a *Must Year*, you occasionally ask, "Compared to earlier this year, how am I actually doing?" rather than only judging yourself by today's state.

Today's Must Reflection

Since the start of this year, what is one clear way your relationship with your body or energy has improved, even slightly?

DAY 312

Career & Financial Well-Being × Direction Over Speed

You may feel pressure to "catch up" financially or professionally, but fast progress in the wrong direction is still misalignment.

In a *Must Year*, you focus less on speed and more on trajectory—whether your current path leads toward the life you want.

Today's Must Reflection

If you stayed on your current money or career path for the next few years, where would it likely take you—and is that where you want to end up?

DAY 313

Love & Intimacy × Patterns Across Time

Patterns in love—how you choose, how you argue, how you withdraw, how you forgive—often repeat across relationships until they're fully acknowledged. Seeing them clearly is the first step toward rewriting them.

In a *Must Year*, you look not only at this relationship, but at the thread that runs through your relationships across time.

Today's Must Reflection

Looking back over your closest romantic relationships (or important connections), what is one pattern in *your* behavior that keeps showing up?

DAY 314

Family, Friends & Community × Shifts This Year

Relational landscapes shift across a year—some ties deepen, others loosen, and some reveal new layers of truth. Noticing these changes helps you relate with intention rather than inertia.

In a Must Year, you ask, "Who moved closer? Who moved further? What does that teach me about where to invest now?"

Today's Must Reflection

Over the past year, which relationship has grown stronger, and which has quietly faded—and what do those shifts tell you?

DAY 315

Career Development & Meaningful Work × Identity Reflection

Identity-based growth focuses on who you are becoming, not only what you produce. Over many months, your sense of self around work or calling may shift in subtle but significant ways.

In a *Must Year*, you pause to name those changes so they can take root.

Today's Must Reflection

Complete this sentence for yourself today: "Compared to earlier this year, I now see myself more as someone who _____."

DAY 316

Personal Growth & Learning × Common Themes

A year often repeats its themes—lessons about boundaries, courage, truth, self-worth, or trust—appearing in different areas until they're integrated.

In a *Must Year*, you stop treating each challenge as isolated and begin asking, "What has this year kept trying to teach me?"

Today's Must Reflection

Looking across the last several months, what is one lesson or theme that seems to keep appearing in different areas of your life?

DAY 317

Spirituality & Inner Peace × Year's Biggest Question

Every year tends to surface one or two deep questions—about identity, meaning, forgiveness, purpose, or belonging. They follow you quietly, shaping your inner life.

In a *Must Year*, you honor these questions without forcing premature answers.

Today's Must Reflection

If you had to name one big spiritual or life question that has followed you this year, what would it be?

DAY 318

Joy, Rest & Renewal × Joy Audit

A year is not measured only by progress but also by joy—moments when you felt alive, playful, connected, or deeply at peace.

In a *Must Year*, you ask whether your year held enough of those moments, and which ones you want more of next.

Today's Must Reflection

What are two or three joyful moments from this year that stand out—and what do they have in common?

DAY 319

Health & Vitality × Letting Go of One Thing

Sometimes the most powerful health move is not adding a new habit but releasing one pattern or obligation that consistently harms your body or drains your energy.

In a *Must Year*, you ask, "If I let go of even one thing, what difference might it make?"

Today's Must Reflection

What is one recurring choice or obligation that clearly hurts your health or energy—and what would it look like to reduce or release it?

DAY 320

Career & Financial Well-Being × Gratitude and Regret

End-of-year reflection around work and money usually includes both gratitude for what served you and regret for what didn't. Honoring both creates clarity.

In a *Must Year*, gratitude grounds you, and regret guides you—not punishes you—into wiser choices ahead.

Today's Must Reflection

Looking at your money and career this year, what is one thing you're genuinely grateful for—and one regret you want to learn from rather than carry as shame?

DAY 321

Love & Intimacy × This Year's Growth

Relationships rarely transform overnight, but over the course of a year you can see real shifts—in how you communicate, how you set boundaries, how you express affection, and how you receive it.

In a *Must Year*, you pause to notice how *you* have grown in the way you show up in love, regardless of anyone else's pace or participation.

Today's Must Reflection

Since earlier this year, how have you become even slightly healthier, clearer, or kinder in your closest relationship?

DAY 322

Family, Friends & Community × Who You Are With Them Now

You're not the same person you were years ago, even if some people still relate to that older version. End-of-year reflection invites the question, "Who am I with them *now*?"

In a *Must Year*, you consider whether your behavior with family and friends reflects your current self—or old habits that no longer fit.

Today's Must Reflection

Choose one relationship. How would you describe the version of yourself that usually shows up there now—and is that who you want to keep being?

DAY 323

Career Development & Meaningful Work × This Year's Clarity

You may not have reached a perfect sense of calling, but you're almost certainly clearer than you were months ago—about what fits, what drains you, what energizes you, and what you're ready to release.

In a *Must Year*, every gain in clarity—even clarity about what you *don't* want—is progress.

Today's Must Reflection

What do you know *now* about your purpose or direction that you did not know at the start of this year?

DAY 324

Personal Growth & Learning × Old You vs. Current You

A powerful lens for reflection is comparing "old you" and "current you" in actual situations—conflict, rest, boundaries, courage, or self-care.

In a *Must Year*, this comparison is not for judgment but for proof that you *are* changing.

Today's Must Reflection

Think of a situation you faced this year that "old you" would have handled very differently. What did you do this time that shows growth?

DAY 325

Spirituality & Inner Peace × This Year's Anchor

Most years reveal an "anchor"—a phrase, practice, prayer, habit, or sense of presence that helped you stay grounded when life pulled at you.

In a *Must Year*, you name this anchor so you can keep or deepen it in the next season.

Today's Must Reflection

What has helped you feel grounded or spiritually steady this year—however simple—and how might you carry it forward?

DAY 326

Joy, Rest & Renewal × Enough Joy?

Looking back, you can ask a truly important question: "Did I allow myself enough joy for a human life this year?"

In a *Must Year*, if the answer is no, that awareness becomes an invitation—not a reason to criticize yourself.

Today's Must Reflection

On a scale of 1–10, how much genuine joy and play did this year include for you—and what number would you like next year to move toward?

DAY 327

Health & Vitality × Identity Shift Summary

Identity-based health change often sounds like: "I used to see myself as someone who ___; now I see myself more as someone who ___."

In a *Must Year*, naming that shift reinforces it.

Today's Must Reflection

Complete this sentence: "Earlier this year I saw myself as someone who _____ with my health, but now I see myself more as someone who _____."

DAY 328

Career & Financial Well-Being × What You're Proud Of

End-of-year reflections often fixate on what's missing. It's equally important to ask, "What, in this area, am I genuinely proud of?"

In a *Must Year*, you acknowledge effort, courage, clarity, and boundaries—not just outcomes.

Today's Must Reflection

What is one money or career decision, boundary, or risk from this year that you are honestly proud of?

DAY 329

Love & Intimacy × One Thing You'd Repeat

Not everything needs to change. Some choices in love were healthy and deserve to be repeated—how you apologized, how you listened, how you honored yourself, how you cared.

In a *Must Year*, you identify not only what needs repair but also what you want to consciously continue.

Today's Must Reflection

In your closest relationship, what is one thing you did this year that you definitely want to repeat going forward?

DAY 330

Family, Friends & Community × 330 Day Gratitude and Intention

After many months, your circle may look different—and so do you. This is a moment for gratitude ("Thank you for…") and intention ("Next year, I want to…").

In a *Must Year*, you let appreciation and honest direction shape how you enter the next season with your people.

Today's Must Reflection

Looking at your current circle, what are you most grateful for—and what is one clear intention you want to bring into your relationships in the coming season?

DAY 331

Health & Vitality × Closing the Gap

There is often a gap between how you *intend* to treat your body and how you do. Over many months, that gap may have narrowed, even if it hasn't disappeared.

In a *Must Year*, you acknowledge both truths: where the gap has closed and where it still needs attention—without collapsing into all-or-nothing thinking.

Today's Must Reflection

Where has the gap between your health intentions and your actual choices gotten smaller this year—and where is it still widest?

DAY 332

Career & Financial Well-Being × Story Rewrite

You carried an existing story into this year—about work, about money, about what's possible for you. Perhaps it was shaped by old fears, past mistakes, or inherited beliefs. Some parts of that story may no longer fit.

In a *Must Year*, you begin rewriting that story consciously, one sentence at a time.

Today's Must Reflection

If you compared your "money/career story" from the start of the year to now, what one sentence would you change?

DAY 333

Love & Intimacy × What You've Learned About Loving

Each year teaches you something about how real love asks you to show up—more honestly, more gently, more courageously, or with clearer boundaries.

In a *Must Year*, you gather those lessons instead of letting them fade.

Today's Must Reflection

What is one key thing you've learned this year about how *you* need to love differently going forward?

DAY 334

Family, Friends & Community × Who Feels Like Home

Not everyone in your life feels like "home." Some people offer ease, safety, understanding, or a sense of being known—and those qualities stand out over time.

In a *Must Year*, you pay attention to who truly feels like home so you can nurture those bonds more intentionally.

Today's Must Reflection

Who are one or two people who most felt like "home" to you this year—and what makes you say that?

DAY 335

Career Development & Meaningful Work × One Degree of Turn

A calling rarely shifts by 180 degrees all at once. More often, it adjusts by a degree or two—small changes in courage, focus, audience, skill, or direction.

In a *Must Year*, you recognize and honor those one-degree turns as the way a life gradually reorients toward purpose.

Today's Must Reflection

If your direction is a compass, what small "degree of turn" did you make this year toward the work you're really meant to do?

DAY 336

Personal Growth & Learning × How You Handle Yourself Now

One of the clearest signs of growth is how you treat yourself when you're tired, afraid, hurt, or disappointed. Over time, your inner tone may have softened, even if not perfectly.

In a *Must Year*, you measure progress not only by achievements but by how you handle yourself now compared to before.

Today's Must Reflection

When you fall short or struggle today, how does your self-talk differ from earlier this year?

DAY 337

Spirituality & Inner Peace × This Year's Shifts in Belief

Your beliefs about meaning, God, humanity, or the sacred may not have flipped, but they may have deepened, softened, clarified, or expanded.

In a *Must Year*, you allow your spiritual understanding to be living, adaptive, and responsive, not fixed in place.

Today's Must Reflection

What is one way your view of what is "sacred" or deeply important has shifted over the course of this year?

DAY 338

Joy, Rest & Renewal × Non-Negotiables

Looking back, you may notice that certain practices—walks, reading, music, creativity, laughter—made a disproportionate difference in how well you coped.

In a *Must Year*, you treat a few of these as non-negotiables, not luxuries.

Today's Must Reflection

Which one or two small pleasures or rest practices, when present, made the biggest positive difference for you this year?

DAY 339

Health & Vitality × Thanking Your Body

Your body has carried you through all of this year—through stress, joy, work, healing, hope, and fatigue—often without receiving a word of gratitude.

In a *Must Year*, you practice speaking to your body with respect for what it has endured and allowed.

Today's Must Reflection

If you were to thank your body for three specific things it has carried you through this year, what would they be?

DAY 340

Career & Financial Well-Being × Setting Up the Next Chapter

Reflection gains its power when it leads to even one clear adjustment in how you spend, save, risk, rest, or pursue your next steps.

In a *Must Year*, you turn insight into intention for the chapter ahead.

Today's Must Reflection

Based on everything you've learned this year, what is one specific, doable change you commit to making in your money or career life going forward?

DAY 341

Health & Vitality × Whole Life View

By now, health is not just about a single habit—it's about how sleep, food, movement, stress, and relationships have supported or strained you across the year.

In a *Must Year*, you zoom out and ask where one small adjustment could create the biggest positive ripple across your whole life.

Today's Must Reflection

Looking at your health this year, what one change had (or could have) the greatest impact across multiple areas of your life?

DAY 342

Career & Financial Well-Being × Identity Statement

Identity-based habits invite you to describe who you are becoming in work and money—not just what you earn or do.

In a *Must Year*, you anchor that identity in a simple, forward-leaning statement you can carry into the next season.

Today's Must Reflection

Complete this sentence: *"I am becoming the kind of person who handles work and money by _____."*

DAY 343

Love & Intimacy × Year's Hardest Moment

Relationships are shaped not only by their best days but by how you navigated the hardest ones—conflict, distance, fear, or heartbreak.

In a *Must Year*, you revisit those moments not to reopen wounds but to understand what they revealed about your needs, limits, and capacity to love well.

Today's Must Reflection

What was the hardest moment in love or intimacy this year—and what did it show you about what you need, or what you cannot continue to accept?

If this reflection brings up intense or overwhelming feelings, consider talking with a qualified mental health or medical professional; you do not have to carry this alone.

DAY 344

Family, Friends & Community × Who You Want to Be to Them

End-of-year reflection is not only about what you received, but about who you chose to be in the lives of your people.

In a *Must Year*, you ask, "What kind of presence do I want to be remembered for?" and let that vision guide your relationships.

Today's Must Reflection

If your family and friends described you in one sentence next year, what would you *want* that sentence to be?

DAY 345

Career Development & Meaningful Work × Three Highlights

Across many ordinary days, a few standout moments likely made you feel deeply aligned with your purpose—however you define it.

In a *Must Year*, you gather those highlights as clues for where to lean more boldly in the future.

Today's Must Reflection

Name three moments this year when you felt most "This is what I'm meant to be doing." What do they have in common?

DAY 346

Personal Growth & Learning × Top Three Lessons

Naming your biggest lessons turns experience into wisdom instead of just memory.

In a *Must Year*, you distill a complex season into a few truths you want to carry forward with intention.

Today's Must Reflection

If you had to name your top three personal lessons from this year, what would they be?

DAY 347

Spirituality & Inner Peace × Guiding Word

Many people choose a word or phrase for the coming year—something that captures how they want to show up in both spiritual and practical life.

In a *Must Year*, you consider a guiding word that can shape your choices, tone, and posture in the next season.

Today's Must Reflection

What single word or short phrase best describes how you want to live and grow in the season ahead?

DAY 348

Joy, Rest & Renewal × Intention for Enjoyment

Joy rarely increases by accident. Even small intentions—more walks, more music, more shared meals—can reshape your calendar and your energy.

In a *Must Year*, you treat enjoyment as part of a Must life, not something separate from it.

Today's Must Reflection

What is one clear intention you want to set around fun, rest, or play for the coming year?

DAY 349

Health & Vitality × Gratitude and Commitment

A healthy way to close a chapter is with both gratitude ("Thank you, body, for…") and commitment ("Next year, I will…").

In a *Must Year*, you honor what has carried you this far and name how you plan to care for it more consciously next year.

Today's Must Reflection

What are you most grateful to your body for this year—and what is one specific way you commit to honoring it more next year?

DAY 350

Career & Financial Well-Being × Looking Ahead with Identity

Identity-based work teaches that each action is a "vote" for the person you are becoming. As this year closes, you choose how you'll vote in the next one.

In a *Must Year*, you ask, "Who do I want to be in work and money a year from now—and what first votes can I cast?"

Today's Must Reflection

Describe, in a few sentences, the version of you handling work and money a year from now—and name two small "votes" you can cast for that person in the next month.

DAY 351

Health & Vitality × What You're Leaving Behind

As a year closes, it helps to name not only what you're keeping but also what you're ready to release—habits, attitudes, or patterns that drain your health and energy.

In a *Must Year*, you consciously decide what doesn't get to travel with you into the next chapter.

Today's Must Reflection

What is one health- or energy-related habit, belief, or pattern you are ready to leave in this year?

DAY 352

Career & Financial Well-Being × Most Valuable Lesson

Every year teaches at least one defining lesson about work or money—about boundaries, courage, fear, worth, or direction.

In a *Must Year*, you name that lesson clearly, so it becomes guidance for the future rather than fading into memory.

Today's Must Reflection

What is the single most valuable lesson this year taught you about work or money—and how will you use it going forward?

DAY 353

Love & Intimacy × What You Want More Of

You've seen what helps love feel safe and alive—certain conversations, time together, affection, honesty, humor, or shared growth.

In a *Must Year*, you ask for more of what strengthens you, not just what you want to avoid.

Today's Must Reflection

In your love life—present or future—what do you clearly want *more* of next year?

DAY 354

Family, Friends & Community × What You're Ready to Release

Some relational roles or expectations have quietly exhausted you—being the fixer, the mediator, the constant host, the emotional sponge, the rescuer.

In a *Must Year*, you decide which roles you are no longer willing to carry in the same way.

Today's Must Reflection

What expectation or role in your family or friendships are you ready to loosen or release so you can be healthier?

DAY 355

Career Development & Meaningful Work × Next Year Intent

Reflection is not only about what happened—it's about what's next. Purpose grows stronger with even one clear, honest intention for the coming season.

In a *Must Year*, you choose a simple focus to guide your direction toward meaningful work.

Today's Must Reflection

What is one realistic, clear intention you want to set for your purpose or calling in the next year?

DAY 356

Personal Growth & Learning × Advice to Earlier You

Looking back, you now know things your earlier self didn't—about boundaries, identity, love, money, courage, or health.

In a *Must Year*, you turn that hindsight into compassion instead of regret.

Today's Must Reflection

If you could speak to yourself at the start of this year, what one piece of advice or encouragement would you give?

DAY 357

Spirituality & Inner Peace × What Helped Most

Some practices, people, or ideas helped you feel grounded this year more than others.

In a *Must Year*, you identify what truly supported your inner peace so you can carry it into hard seasons ahead.

Today's Must Reflection

Looking back, what most helped your inner peace or spiritual life this year—and how can you prioritize it again?

DAY 358

Joy, Rest & Renewal × What You'll Intentionally Add

Instead of vaguely wishing that "next year will be lighter," you choose a concrete form of joy or rest to include on purpose.

In a *Must Year*, you treat these additions as part of your plan for a better life—not as extras.

Today's Must Reflection

What specific activity, practice, or rhythm of fun or rest do you want to *add* into your life next year?

DAY 359

Health & Vitality × Gratitude for Change

Even if progress felt slow, you are not standing in the exact place you were months ago. Small shifts count and deserve acknowledgement.

In a *Must Year*, you thank yourself for the changes you made instead of minimizing them.

Today's Must Reflection

What are two health or energy changes—however small—you're genuinely grateful you made this year?

DAY 360

Whole Life Integration × Year Compass

End-of-year frameworks like the Wheel of Life often point toward one central question: *"Given everything I've seen this year, who am I choosing to be now?"*

In a *Must Year*, you gather your reflections into a simple, intentional direction—not a list of regrets.

Today's Must Reflection

In one or two sentences, how would you describe the person you are choosing to be as you step into the next chapter of your life?

DAY 361

Love & Intimacy × Who You Are as a Partner

By now, you have a clearer sense of how you show up in love—what you do well, where you avoid, how you repair, and what you need. That awareness is part of your Must identity.

In a Must Year, you move from "I hope love works out" to "I am actively shaping the kind of partner I am becoming."

Today's Must Reflection

If you described yourself as a partner (present or future) in three honest words, what would they be now—and what one word would you like to grow into next?

DAY 362

Family, Friends & Community × Circle of Choice

You began life in circles you didn't choose. Over time, you added people by choice and adjusted distance with others. Your current "circle of choice" reflects your values as much as your habits.

In a *Must Year*, you recognize that curating who is close to you is part of protecting who you are becoming.

Today's Must Reflection

Looking at the people closest to you now, what do they reflect back about your values—and is there anyone you need a little closer or a little further away?

DAY 363

Career Development & Meaningful Work × Must Identity

The heart of this year has been shifting from "I have goals" to "I have a Must identity"—someone who lives in alignment with what truly matters, even imperfectly.

In a *Must Year*, you stop seeing purpose as a distant destination and begin owning it as who you are on ordinary days.

Today's Must Reflection

Complete this sentence honestly and boldly: **"I am someone who is meant to _____ in this world."**

DAY 364

Whole Life Integration × From Year to Way of Life

You called this a *Must Year*, but the point was never just twelve months. The real win is that pieces of this way of living have become part of you—how you reflect, decide, relate, and recover.

In a Must life, you carry forward what kept you honest and aligned, instead of treating this journey as a one-time project.

Today's Must Reflection

Which three practices or mindsets from this year do you commit to carrying forward—not just for a season, but as part of your ongoing way of life?

DAY 365

Closing the Circle × Beginning Again

You have walked through 365 days of looking at your life with clearer eyes and a kinder, truer heart. The outer details may still be in motion, but your relationship with yourself, your story, and your future has changed.

In a *Must Year*, the last day is not an ending; it is a handoff—from this guided journey to the person you have become, who is now capable of guiding themselves with more courage, clarity, and compassion.

Today's Must Reflection

As you stand at Day 365, what promise do you want to make to yourself about how you will treat your life, your time, and your identity from this day forward?

Quarter 4 – Closing and Beginning

You are entering the final stretch of your *Must Year*.

This quarter has invited you to:

- Review your health, money, relationships, and inner life at year scale.
- Name what you are grateful for and what you regret.
- Decide what you are leaving behind and what you are carrying forward.
- Articulate who you are choosing to be from here.

Quarter 4 is about **closure and commitment**. Not a neat, perfect ending—but an honest accounting and a chosen direction.

Look back over Days 271–360. Pay attention to:

- Entries where you used "this year" language ("This year, I…," "Compared to earlier…")
- Your words around gratitude, release, intention, and identity.

Season 4 Reflection

Use these questions to help you gather the year:

1. If you had to describe this *Must Year* in one sentence, what would it be?
2. What are three changes—internal or external—that you are genuinely grateful for?
3. What are two patterns you now understand much better, even if they are not fully resolved?

4. What is one thing you know you are **done** carrying into the next chapter?

5. What is one promise you are making to yourself about how you will treat your life, your time, and your identity from now on?

You are almost at Day 365, but there is no real "after" to this work. The point of this year was never to complete a book; it was to learn a way of being in conversation with your own life.

As you move into the final pages, hold this in mind:

You are not graduating from your Must life.
You are stepping more fully into it.

A YEAR-END LETTER

You have reached the last page, but you have not reached the end.

Whenever you began this journey—January 1, or a random Tuesday—you opened to Day 1 with more questions than answers. Across these pages, you have examined how you treat your body, your money, your work, your people, your rest, your faith, and yourself. You have named losses and desires. You have challenged old stories and written new ones. Whether you touched every page or only some, you spent real, meaningful time in honest conversation with your own life.

And that matters.

What Has Changed (Even If You Missed Days)

Change rarely arrives with a trumpet. It shows up quietly:

- You pause before saying yes.
- You soften the tone of your self-talk.
- You notice when you are reacting from an old wound instead of the present moment.

- You recognize patterns in health, money, love, and work that once felt random.
- You feel more responsible for who you are becoming—and less at the mercy of circumstances.

The outer details of life may still be unfolding. But your *relationship* to those details is not the same. You now tell yourself the truth without abandoning yourself in the process. That is real transformation.

If you doubt this, flip through your own writing. The evidence is there.

Who You Are Now

This book was never about becoming a flawless version of yourself. It was about becoming more *fully* yourself:

- Someone who can see clearly and still choose hope.
- Someone who can set a boundary without shutting down love.
- Someone who can handle money, health, work, and faith with more honesty and less shame.
- Someone who can fail, apologize, reset, and still remember their worth.

You are not finished.
You are *more awake*.

Your Must identity is not a destination.
It is a way you walk now.

Where You Go From Here

There is no rule that says you must "start over" tomorrow. But you may choose to. You now have several paths:

- **Repeat the year with new eyes.**

The same questions will meet a different you.

- **Create your own Must rhythm.**

    Revisit domains monthly—health, money, love, rest, purpose.

- **Translate reflection into plans.**

    Let what you've learned shape concrete changes in the coming months.

- **Share Must with safe people.**

    Without revealing private writing, bring key questions into your relationships.

You no longer need a book to know how to ask yourself honest questions. You have practiced that for 365 days.

A Promise Forward

The most important commitment now is not to a specific goal but to a way of relating to your life:

- To tell yourself the truth, kindly.
- To adjust your days to match what you value.
- To treat your time, body, gifts, and relationships as things that matter.
- To live as if your life is a Must— because it is.

This book has been a companion along the way.
Close the cover knowing the companion now lives inside you.

Every day from here is not just another date on a calendar.
It is another line in the story of your Must life.

And *you* hold the pen.

THANK YOU, AND NEXT STEPS

If this book has encouraged or helped you, **would you take a moment to leave a review**? Your feedback makes a real difference and helps other readers discover this work. You can share your thoughts on Amazon.com, Goodreads.com, Barnes & Noble, or your preferred bookseller, and consider sharing or gifting this book to someone who might benefit from it. To continue your journey, visit **MustYear.com** and **StephenRue.Live** for more resources, events, and tools in the Must Personal Development series.

Thank you for being part of this work and for supporting these books.

ACKNOWLEDGMENTS

With deep gratitude, I thank my family for their unwavering love, encouragement, and belief in me. I also honor my personal development mentors—Brian Tracy, Les Brown, Jack Canfield, and Tony Robbins—whose teachings have profoundly shaped my thinking and practice. Finally, I acknowledge the ancient and contemporary luminaries who have explored human potential and meaning; their timeless wisdom echoes throughout these pages.

IF YOU WANT TO GO FURTHER: THE MUST PERSONAL DEVELOPMENT SERIES

Your Must journey does not end on Day 365. If anything, this year has prepared you for a deeper, more aligned way of living.

The **Must Personal Development Series** is an expanding collection of books designed to support your growth across identity, goals, habits, relationships, purpose, and daily life. Each title builds on the others, but every one can also stand alone.

Here is how the current books work together:

Must: Becoming the Person You Are Meant to Be

Your foundation.

This is where you uncover your Must Identity, challenge old narratives, strengthen your values and standards, and step into who you were always meant to be.

Must Goals: The Art and Science of Authentic Goal-Setting for Lasting Change

Your method.

This book shows you how to create goals rooted in identity rather than pressure or performance, using the I AM SMART TO ACT™ framework and research-backed tools for lasting change.

The Must Book Guided Journal

Your weekly integration.

A structured space to reflect, align, and live your Must Identity every week of the year.

Must Year (this book)

Your daily practice.

A yearlong journey of reflection, alignment, and honest inner work—365 touchpoints that keep you grounded in who you are becoming.

Together, these books form the Must Pathway:

Identity → Goals → Weekly Integration → Daily Practice → Whole-Life Transformation

The Must Personal Development Series will continue to grow with future releases.

For the most current list of books, resources, tools, and updates, visit:

MustYear.com/Resources

RECOMMENDED READING AND RESOURCES

For updated reading lists, research notes, downloadable tools, **online Companion Journal**, and future releases in the **Must Personal Development Series**, visit:

MustYear.com/Resources

This page serves as a living, evolving library to support your ongoing journey.

ABOUT THE AUTHOR

Stephen Rue is an award-winning, bestselling author and personal development expert whose diverse life and professional experience fuel his mission to help people transform their lives. A renowned lawyer and counselor-at-law licensed in multiple states, he holds a BBA from Southern Methodist University, a law degree, and an MBA from Loyola University, has completed leadership training at Harvard Law School, and is pursuing a doctorate at National University. Voted "Best Attorney" in New Orleans, Stephen is known for bringing the same tenacity, compassion, and strategic thinking from the courtroom into his personal development work.

Certified as a trauma recovery life coach, Stephen draws on his own journey of overcoming family tragedy and personal hardship to help others heal, reset, and rise. For decades, he has guided thousands of clients and readers to flourish through a rare blend of legal advocacy, mindset work, and practical tools for change. His zest for life extends beyond his professional roles—he has reigned as a Mardi Gras King. He is also an author, motivational speaker, artist, sculptor, and marathon runner, embodying the creative, disciplined life he teaches.

The Must Personal Development Series—*Must: Becoming the Person You Are Meant to Be*, the *Must Book Guided Journal, Must Goals,* and *Must Year*—distills more than thirty years of Stephen's study and research across psychology, neuroscience, philosophy, and personal growth into a clear, actionable roadmap for transformation. His approach combines academic rigor with real-world application, making complex ideas simple, usable, and deeply relevant to everyday life. Through his writing, speaking, and one-on-one work, Stephen equips readers with the mindset, habits, and goal systems to navigate adversity and become the person they are meant to be.

www.ingramcontent.com/pod-product-compliance
Lightning Source LLC
Chambersburg PA
CBHW032029150426
43194CB00006B/208